Praise for *Jesus*

"Like Anita Diamant with *The Red Tent*, Deepak Chopra has written about a Bible story in the form of a Jewish midrash, filling in the blanks in the biblical narrative about Jesus's life. A la *The Da Vinci Code*, this thought-provoking tale is sure to ignite exciting questions and controversy."

—Jill Gregory, coauthor of the international bestseller *The Book of Names* and the forthcoming thriller *The Illumination*

"It is such an original and intriguing approach to imagine which Jesus was 'left out of the Bible.' Chopra's novel is a fascinating read."

—Petru Popescu, author of the forthcoming *Girl Mary*

"In *Jesus: A Story of Enlightenment*, Deepak Chopra dares us to ponder paradigms imbedded deep within our very DNA and to question unquestionable truths. Chopra introduces a breathtaking epistemology that is altogether fresh and divine. His powerful revelation threatens our ability to live our lives in darkness."

—Cheryl Woodcock, correspondent and producer, *Entertainment Tonight* and *The Insider*

"As a Jew I was taught to reject Jesus. As a mystic I was drawn to his light. This brave book invites me to approach Jesus anew, with great curiosity and a humble heart, and to love him, in the end, as my Self."

—Raphael Cushnir, author of *The One Thing Holding You Back*

"Deepak Chopra has turned his profound gifts of insight and communication into creating a novel, *Jesus: A Story of Enlightenment.* But it is no ordinary novel, and in the closing sections his thought-provoking questions will cause us to reflect in ways we may never have done before. It's the problem of a Jesus we never really knew, and of a gospel that apparently never came true, or more accurately that demands more of human nature than Christians have in the main ever been willing to give. If you think all that could be said about Jesus has already been said, then this book will be an eye-opener in the best and truest sense of those words. Do a major favor to your soul and read it."

—Miceal Ledwith, L.Ph., L.D., D.D., LL.D, was formerly a Professor of Systematic Theology and University President, and for seventeen years was a member of the Vatican's International Theological Commission

"We journey with a very human Jesus through a tough and turbulent landscape to discover his greatest message, that of personal transformation and enlightenment. Deepak Chopra's story is an inspiring gift for those who truly care and have the courage to seek."

—Michael Baigent, author of *The Jesus Papers*

JESUS

JESUS

A STORY OF ENLIGHTENMENT

DEEPAK CHOPRA

HarperOne
An Imprint of HarperCollins*Publishers*

HarperOne

HarperCollins books may be purchased for educational, business, or sales promotional use. For information please write: Special Markets Department, HarperCollins Publishers, 10 East 53rd Street, New York, NY 10022.

HarperCollins Web site: http://www.harpercollins.com
HarperCollins®, ®, and HarperOne™ are
trademarks of HarperCollins Publishers.

FIRST HARPERCOLLINS PAPERBACK EDITION PUBLISHED IN 2009
Designed by Level C

Library of Congress Cataloging-in-Publication Data

Chopra, Deepak.
Jesus : a story of enlightenment / Deepak Chopra.—1st ed.
p. cm.
ISBN 978-0-06-144874-4
1. Jesus Christ—Fiction. I. Title.
PS3553.H587J47 2008
813'.54—dc22 2008051465

10 11 12 13 RRD (H) 10 9 8 7 6 5

CONTENTS

PART THREE
MESSIAH

AUTHOR'S NOTE

This book isn't about the Jesus found in the New Testament, but the Jesus who was left out. The gospel writers are silent about "the lost years," as they are known, covering the span in Jesus's life between the ages of twelve and thirty. Jesus actually disappears before that, however, since the only incident reported after the birth narratives is the one (given only in the gospel of Luke) in which the twelve-year-old Jesus gets separated from his parents during Passover in Jerusalem. Joseph and Mary are already on the road home before they realize what has happened. Anxiously they retrace their steps and find their son Yeshua (as he was known in Hebrew) discussing God with priests in the Temple. Except for that one striking mention, Jesus's childhood and youth are more or less a blank.

Yet there's another Jesus left out of the New Testament—the enlightened Jesus. His absence, in my view, has profoundly crippled the Christian faith, for as unique as Christ is, making him the one and only Son of God leaves the rest of humankind stranded. A huge abyss separates Jesus's holiness from our ordinariness. Millions of Christians accept this separation, but it doesn't have to exist. What if Jesus wanted his followers—and us—to reach the same unity with God that he had reached?

My story is based on the premise that he did. By following the young seeker from Nazareth on his path to Christhood, I've laid out a map of enlightenment. It wasn't necessary to invent the map. Enlightenment has existed in every age. The path from suffering and separation to bliss and unity with God is well marked. I put Jesus on this path because I believe he walked it. Of course, any number of confirmed Christians will disagree, sometimes violently. They want Jesus to remain unique, the only man who was also God. But if Jesus belongs to the world, as I believe he does, his story can't exclude everyone else who has realized God-consciousness. In this novel Jesus remains a savior, but he isn't *the* savior.

I didn't feel comfortable at first tackling a novel about the lost years. It's not conceivable to write a new scripture, and if you decide instead to present Jesus in a secular tone, you run the risk of denying his sacred role, which is absolutely real. I wanted to give believing Christians—and all seekers—even more reasons to be inspired. To do that, Jesus has to be brought into the scheme of everyday life. He worries about violence and unrest; he wonders if God is listening; he is intensely absorbed in the question, "Who am I?" My intention was in no way to contradict Jesus's teachings in the Bible, but rather to imagine how he arrived at them.

So what does Jesus look like as a young, doubting seeker? I wrestled with several possibilities. I could have pretended that this was a lost biography. But biographies need to be based on fact, and in this case we know few facts: the names of Jesus's family and scarcely anything else. Could Jesus read? How educated was he in the Torah? Did he live apart from Roman culture or mix freely with the imperial colonists and soldiers? No one can answer with any certainty.

Recent scholarship even disputes whether Jesus was a carpenter; some authorities claim that his father, Joseph, was more likely a stonemason or general "handworker," as such jacks-of-all-trades were called. In any event, the New Testament isn't biographical either. It's a partisan argument for why a certain charismatic wanderer was actually the long-awaited messiah, and it was written in turbulent times when other candidates for messiahship were making their case just as loudly.

Another possibility was to write a kind of spiritual fantasy, allowing my imagination to run free. Spiritual fantasies have no limits, since there are no facts to hold them in check. Jesus could train in a magician's workshop in Ephesus or visit the Parthenon to sit at the feet of Plato's heirs. But this course seemed presumptuous.

Finally, I could have taken the familiar and beloved Jesus of the gospels and worked backwards. That would have been the safest course, a kind of *Young Indiana Jones* that whets our appetite for the hero we know is coming. If the gospels show us a man full of love, compassion, kindness, and wisdom, it's only plausible that he would have started out as a child who preternaturally displayed love, kindness, compassion, and wisdom. Over the years these traits would have blossomed until the day came, around age thirty, when Christ burst on the scene, asking his cousin John to baptize him in the river Jordan.

By revolving all these possibilities in my mind, I realized that more than one Jesus has been left out of the Bible. It only made sense to restore the one that's most crucial, the pivotal Jesus that begs to be known. For me, he's not a person, but a state of consciousness. How Jesus came to be united with God was a process that happened in the mind. Seen from the perspective of Buddha or the ancient rishis ("seers") of India, Jesus attained enlightenment. This was my true subject. A youth with the potential to be a savior discovered his potential and then learned to fulfill it.

I hope I can satisfy readers' deepest curiosity. What does union with God feel like? Can Jesus's path also be ours? I believe it can. Jesus was a teacher of higher consciousness, not just a shining example of it. He told his disciples that they would do everything he could do and more. He called them the "light of the world," the same term he applied to himself. He pointed toward the Kingdom of Heaven as an eternal state of grace, not a faraway place hidden above the clouds.

In short, the Jesus who is left out of the New Testament turns out to be in many ways the most important Jesus for modern times. His aspiration to find salvation vibrates in every heart. If it didn't, the brief career of a controversial, largely despised rabbi on the outskirts of first-century Jewish society wouldn't mean much. Yet as we all know, that obscure rabbi became imbedded forever in myth and symbol. I didn't want the Jesus in this book to be worshiped, much less to push him forward as definitive. The events of the tale are pure fiction. But at a deeper level Jesus feels real to me because I've gotten a glimpse into his mind. One flash of insight answers many prayers. I hope readers feel the same way.

Deepak Chopra
May 2008

JESUS

PART ONE

SEEKER

1

THE STRANGER IN THE SNOW

A horse!" the temple lad cried as he ran in panting for breath. "Quick, come and see."

"Why?" I asked without looking up. I was in the middle of writing, which I did every morning. My scribbles never reached anyone outside this dim, falling-down hut, but that's of no matter.

"Because he's huge. Hurry, or somebody might steal him."

"Before you do, you mean?"

The boy was so excited that he kept sloshing his bucket of hot water on the floor. He was permitted to barge into the hut to fill my bath just after dawn.

I frowned at him. "What about detachment?"

"What?" he asked.

"I thought the priest was teaching you not to get so excited."

"That was before the horse."

If you were born high in these mountains, a stray horse is an event. Where would this one be from? The Western empire probably, where huge black stallions are bred. The locals knew animals by the compass. Elephants come from the south, where the jungle begins, and camels from the eastern desert. In all my travels, I had seen only one of these gray monsters, who are like walking walls.

From the north, over the passes, came small, furry ponies, and these were very common—traders used ponies to reach the villages with their goods: hemp, silk, incense, salt, dried meat, and flour. The bare necessities plus the silk to adorn a bride in joy or wrap a corpse in sorrow.

I set the ink-laden brush back on its stand and rubbed the black from my fingers. "You'd better put that bucket down before you drown us both," I said. "Then fetch my cloak."

Outside, a storm had swooped down off the high peaks overnight, batting at the stretched animal skins over my windows and leaving another foot of fresh snow. I emerged from the hut and looked around.

More than a horse is here, I thought.

The temple lad couldn't stand to wait for me and rushed down the trail.

"Find the stranger," I shouted.

The boy whirled around. I was calling with the wind, and at these altitudes my voice could be heard at a long distance.

"What stranger?" the boy called back.

"The one who fell off the horse. Search for him. Search hard, and don't dawdle."

The temple lad hesitated. He much preferred gawking at a fine huge horse, but finding a body in the snow had its own appeal. He nodded and turned the corner out of sight. The boulders on either side of the trail were large enough for a grown man to disappear into, much less a scrawny boy.

I proceeded slowly after him, but not because of age. I don't know how old I am. The matter lost its interest long ago. But I can still move without creaking.

I had foreseen the mysterious stranger two days earlier, but not the overnight storm. The snow wouldn't kill him, but the blast of frigid air that howled off the peaks most likely would. Nobody from the world below anticipates that kind of cold. I've helped the villagers rescue the stranded travelers who were fortunate. Only their noses and toes were blackened. They were numb at first after being dragged to shelter, but started screaming with pain as soon as the rescuers warmed them up.

Everyone in my valley has enormous respect for the high peaks and their dangers. But they also revere the mountains, which remind them of how close Heaven is. I don't need the comfort of Heaven.

The villagers didn't call on me for rescue work anymore. It disturbed them that an old ascetic who looked like a crooked teak carving could trek in his bare feet when theirs were bound in layers of goatskin and rags. Huddling on long winter nights, they discussed this, and they decided that I had made a pact with a demon. Since there were thousands of local demons, a few could be spared to look after my feet.

I walked down the trail until I heard a faint distant sound in the wind, more like a rodent squeak than a boy's voice. But I understood its meaning. I veered left where the sound came from and hurried my steps. I had a personal interest in finding the stranger alive.

What I found when I came over the next ridge was a mound in the snow. The temple lad was staring at the mound, which didn't move.

"I waited for you before kicking it," he said. His face held that mixture of dread and relish that comes over people when they think they've discovered a corpse.

"Listen to me. Don't wish him dead. It doesn't help," I warned.

Instead of kicking at the mound, the lad knelt and began to sweep it furiously with his hands. The stranger had managed to bury himself under a foot-thick layer of snow, but that wasn't as surprising as something else. When I finally saw his outlined body, the man was crouched on his knees with clasped hands folded under his chin. The boy had never seen anyone in that posture before.

"Did he seize up like that?" he asked.

I didn't reply. As I gazed at the body, it impressed me that someone could remain praying to the point of death. The position also told me that this was a Jew, because as you travel east, holy men sit cross-legged when they pray; they don't kneel.

I told the boy to run down to the village for a sledge, and he obeyed without question. In truth the two of us could have carried the body out on our own. But I needed to be alone. As soon as the temple lad had disappeared, I brought my mouth close to the stranger's ear, which was still bright pink although covered with frost.

"Stir yourself," I whispered. "I know who you are."

For a moment nothing happened. To all appearances the stranger remained frozen, but I didn't embrace him to give him warmth from my own body. If this was the visitor I was expecting, it wasn't necessary. But I granted one small concession. I called the stranger by name.

"Jesus, awaken."

Most souls will respond when you call their name. A few will come to you even from the shadow of death. The stranger stirred, faintly at first, just enough to shake a dusting of snowflakes from his frost-matted hair. It wasn't a question of thawing out. Humans aren't like carp, which can be seen suspended in the ice all winter, only to wriggle back to life when the lakes unfreeze in spring. The stranger had willed himself into total stillness and now willed himself out again. If I had let the boy witness it, he would have been convinced that I was performing black magic.

Jesus lifted his head and stared blankly. He wasn't quite back in the world. I gradually came into focus.

"Who are you?" he asked.

"It doesn't matter," I replied.

I tried to help him to his feet. Jesus resisted. "I came only to see one man. If you're not him, leave me." He was sinewy and strong, even after such an arduous journey, and his resistance pushed me back on my heels.

Jesus didn't ask about his horse. The tongue he spoke was coarse Greek, the kind used in the marketplace of the Western empire. He must have picked it up on his journeys. I knew some Greek, learned from traders when I was about the stranger's age, twenty-five or so.

"Don't be stubborn," I said. "I came and dug you out. Who else would bother with an ordinary mound of snow?"

Jesus remained wary. "How did you find out my name?"

"Your question answers itself," I said. "The right man would know your name without asking."

Now Jesus smiled, and together we forced his knees to unbend from the cold. He stood up shakily, then immediately fell against my shoulder.

"A moment," he said.

In that moment I took his measure. I stood half a head taller than the mountain villagers, and Jesus was that much taller than me. He wore his dark hair and beard cropped, not trimmed neatly but rough, as a traveler will do when there's no time for niceties. His brown eyes seemed darker than usual against his pale skin. Pale, one should say, compared with being sun-baked at altitude, where everyone looks like a leather wineskin.

Jesus allowed me to half carry him up the mountain against my shoulder, which told me that he trusted me now. He didn't ask my name again. A subtle thing, but I took it as a sign of foreknowledge. I prefer strict anonymity. If you want perfect solitude, don't give out your name and never ask anyone else's. The local villagers didn't know my name even after years of proximity, and I forgot theirs as soon as I heard them, even the temple lad's. Sometimes I called him "Cat," because the boy's job was to catch the field rats attracted inside the temple by incense and oil.

After half a mile Jesus straightened up and walked on his own. A moment later he broke his silence. "I've heard of you by reputation. They say you know everything."

"No, they don't. They say I'm a stumbling idiot or a demon worshiper. Tell the truth. You saw me in a vision."

Jesus looked surprised.

I said, "You don't have to hide your knowledge from me." I gave Jesus a look. "Nothing in me is hidden. If you have eyes, you'll see."

He nodded. The trust between us was now complete.

Soon we reached my wind-battered hut. Once inside, I reached up into the rafters and brought down a packet wrapped in dirty linen rags.

"Tea," I said. "The real thing, not the dried barley stalks they boil up around here."

I put a pot of melted snow on the brazier to boil. It made a smoky heat, because for everyday purposes I burned dried dung for fuel. The floor of the hut was plastered with the same dung mixed with straw. Women came in every spring to put down a fresh layer.

Jesus squatted on the floor like a peasant and watched. If I really knew everything, I'd know whether Jesus had learned to sit that way among his people or on his long travels. After the pure air outside, my visitor's eyes watered from the smoke. I pulled aside one of the dried skins covering the window to let in a breeze.

"One gets used to it," I said.

I had no plans to write down this visit, even though I'd had only a handful like it in twenty years. To look at him, there was nothing special about Jesus. The superstition of the ignorant must make giants and monsters out of those with special destinies. Reality is otherwise. Were the eyes of Jesus as deep as the ocean and as dark as eternity? No. To the initiated there was something in his gaze that words couldn't express, but the same is true of a desperately poor village girl seeing her newborn baby for the first time and bursting with love. One soul is every soul; only we refuse to see it.

By the same logic, all words are the words of God. People refuse to see that too. Jesus spoke like everyone else. But not everyone else spoke like Jesus, which is a mystery.

That first hour the two of us drank our black tea, brewed properly and strong in the visitor's honor, not weak the way I usually had it. My supply had to last all winter.

"I think I understand your problem," I said.

"You mean my reason for coming to find you?" asked Jesus.

"They're the same thing, aren't they? You found God, and it wasn't enough. It never is. There's no hunger worse than eternal hunger."

Jesus didn't look surprised. The right man would talk like this, without asking preliminary questions. As for me, I'd seen my share of feverish young men who came up the mountain with their visions. They burned out and left very quickly, taking their visions in ashes with them.

"It's one thing to find God," I said. "It's another to become God. Isn't that what you want?"

Jesus looked startled. Unlike the other feverish young men, he had found me not by his own will, but by being guided invisibly, held by the hand like a child.

"I wouldn't put it that way," he said soberly.

"Why not? You can't be worrying about blasphemy, not at this point." I laughed; it came out as a short, soft bark. "You've already had the word 'blasphemy' thrown at you a hundred times. Don't worry. Nobody's looking over your shoulder. When I shut the door, even the local gods have to keep out."

"Not mine."

After that exchange we didn't talk anymore, but sat silently as the teapot hissed on the brazier. Silence isn't a blank. It's the pregnant possibility of what is about to be born. Silence is the mystery I deal in. Silence and light. So I had no trouble recognizing the light that Jesus brought with him.

There was more, though. This one's road had been laid out before he was born. He was still young and had only caught a glimpse of it. But another might be able to see your whole road without tears. That was the reason Jesus had been guided through the snowstorm, to weave our two visions together.

He fell asleep sitting there, overcome with exhaustion. The next morning he began to tell his story to me. As the words poured out, the cold and dark of the hut made the tale seem unreal. But that was to be expected. Jesus long ago suspected that he might be living in a dream.

I heard his tale and saw much more in my mind. Listen to the story and judge for yourself.

2

THE TWO JUDASES

The booming voice filled the stone granary up to the rafters.

"What's it going to be, brothers? The next time soldiers come marching into your village, are you going to be like the snake, which bites when it is stepped on? Or like the turtle, which hides in its shell, praying that it won't be crushed underfoot?"

The speaker paused; he knew that fear ruled these Galileans. Although no taller than his listeners, he stood straight, while they hunched over like dogs waiting to be whipped. He stamped his foot, raising a cloud of chaff that glowed a dull gold by lantern light.

"You all know me by reputation," he said. "I am Simon, the son of Judas of Galilee. What does that mean to you?"

"It means you're a killer," a voice called from the shadows. The granary was dark except for a single covered lantern. The Romans paid their informants well, and it was an offense punishable by death for rebels to gather in secret.

"Killer?" Simon scoffed. "I make righteous sacrifice."

"You murder priests," the same voice said.

Simon squinted to try to make him out more clearly in the dark. For every dozen men who dared to sneak off to a meeting, rarely even one actually joined the rebel cause. This night's group huddled in an abandoned granary on the outskirts of Nazareth was no different. The Zealot's tone grew harder.

"Murder is against God's law. We eliminate collaborators. Whoever collaborates with Rome is an enemy of the Jews. An enemy of the Jews is an enemy of God. Do you deny this?"

Nobody called out a reply this time. Simon despised their timidity, but he also needed them. They were remote villagers haunted by the specter of starvation. Four out of ten children died before they were five. Families scratched out a bare living in the hills among twisted olive trees and parched wheat fields. It was the only existence they knew.

The man who had called Simon a murderer wasn't Jesus, but Jesus was there. He stood next to his brother James, who was eager to join the rebels. They had argued about attending all morning.

"Just come and listen," James had urged. "You don't have to do anything."

Jesus replied, "Going to their meetings is the same as doing something."

Which was true as far as the Romans were concerned. But when James threatened to go without him, it was Jesus's duty as older brother to come along. The stone granary was cold at night. It smelled of straw and rats' nests.

Simon raised his hands in conciliation. "I know, all you want is to be left in peace, and I am bringing you a sword, the sword of Judas my father. You call us the 'knife men'? Knives are only the beginning."

With a dramatic flourish he pulled a legionary's blade out from under his cloak. Simon could hear suppressed gasps. Even by the glimmer of a covered lantern they could tell that it was Roman steel. He held it high.

"Are we so afraid that just the sight of an enemy's weapon makes us want to piss ourselves? No soldier dropped this sword. It wasn't forgotten in a tavern after a drunken brawl. This was taken in hand-to-hand combat. By one of us . . . by a Jew."

He stepped forward to the nearest man. "Go ahead, touch it, smell it. I've left enemy blood on it." He raised his voice, staring hard at the men in the room. "Everyone touch it."

Jesus grabbed at his brother's arm. "Let's go."

"No!" James whispered, but his tone was fierce. Neither of them had ever laid hands on a sword. The only metal they knew was either a plowshare or a workman's ax and chisel. Now the sword was coming closer.

"If you touch it now, can you ever untouch it?" Jesus asked. At the age of twenty, he had been considered a man for five years, but none of his brothers listened to him.

Simon watched with satisfaction as the weapon was passed around. A Roman sword was his strongest ploy. Rough hands could grasp what simple minds couldn't. He wasn't telling the truth about it, though—the sword had in fact been left behind in a tavern in Damascus and sold to the underground. The blood smeared on it was rabbit's blood that he applied every few days, when he could trap one for dinner. But he had to tell these people something to stir them up. Whether they joined or ran away, they'd remember the sight of a captured sword with enemy blood.

Jesus was one of those who remembered. And he chose the details of this night as the beginning of the story he told me.

He was standing nervously at the back of the group. He wasn't afraid to be there with a Zealot rebel, but he wanted James, his impetuous younger brother, to be afraid, for his own good.

The sword had reached them, and James handed it to Jesus. "Take it," he whispered. The blade was heavier than it looked, short and snub-nosed in shape, which marked it as the weapon of a common foot soldier.

Jesus had seen stolen daggers since he was a boy, and occasionally a Roman scabbard or helmet. Looting from the occupiers was guaranteed to gain respect from other boys. He suspected that the sword was loot and not a battle prize.

"Bring it here," Simon ordered.

Jesus hadn't realized that he was the last in line. He tried to pass the sword over the head of the farmer in front of him.

"No, you bring it," the Zealot said.

Jesus did as he was told, keeping his eyes lowered.

This attempt to seem inconspicuous failed. "I want to see you after everyone else is gone," Simon murmured in a low voice, fixing Jesus in his gaze.

Nobody heard exactly what he said, and James could hardly wait to find out. Jesus refused to satisfy his curiosity. There was only one way out of the granary, and Simon blocked it when the group disbanded. His short, squat, powerful body was as impassable as a boulder.

"I know you," Simon said. "You are sons of David." This was the kind of exaggerated flattery that worked with simple peasants.

Instead, Jesus said, "King's sons don't meet secretly in a barn. Why do you single us two out?"

"Because I have eyes to see. These others are Jews in name only, but you're not."

"See what you will," said Jesus. He could sense his younger brother growing excited and angry.

James burst out, "They're dying in our village every day. Why aren't the rebels doing something about it?"

"What's killing them?" said Simon.

"The Romans bleed us for taxes; we hardly had food for ourselves to begin with."

Simon smiled. An opening. This was the moment that justified his hard, clandestine life. The rebels kept on the move throughout the occupied lands of Palestine, sleeping in barns or behind haystacks. Rarely did a farmer actually take a Zealot in. That risked having his house burned to the ground in retaliation.

Simon said, "You've got good questions. My father can answer them. Would you like to meet him? I can take you there tonight."

James immediately wanted to seize the offer. Simon's father, Judas of Galilee, was the soul of the rebellion. Black-haired as a bear, he came from Gamala, a village no bigger than Nazareth, five hundred people at most. Since he was born, James had seen the Zealots rise out of the ground like ghosts, striking everywhere, even inside the Temple in Jerusalem. But they weren't ghosts. They were the children of Judas's brain, and the arms of his will.

Simon saw the young man's eyes flick nervously toward his older brother, who remained unmoved. "Judas is the greatest man alive, successor to the prophets," James boasted.

The older brother spoke up. "Do we need another prophet of doom? That well's not running dry. It fills back up every generation."

"Look around. The Jews have already met their doom," said Simon. "We don't need a prophet to tell us that. We need one who can win our freedom—my father. Unless you are still dreaming of the messiah, who is always coming tomorrow."

The older brother was stubborn. "You call your father our savior. What kind of savior uses destruction to end destruction?" he said.

Jesus didn't need to explain his meaning. The Zealots had recently stepped up their campaign of terror. Their "knife men" had assassinated several high-ranking priests in Jerusalem, and now they threatened to murder any Jew who cooperated with the Romans, down to the poorest farmer.

Simon spread his hands. "I won't argue with you. Come see for yourself. My father is hidden where the occupiers will never find him. He's safer to visit than this place."

He could feel the younger one wavering, but he was barely fifteen. It was the older one who would be the catch, if he could be won over.

Jesus hesitated. He knew that if he refused the invitation, James would never forgive him. The Zealots had bitterly divided the community. For every Jew who saw them as merciless killers, another saw them as heroes against the oppressor. James was leaning toward the second camp and would likely run off to join them if Jesus stood in his way. Then there was the law. The law of Moses did not forbid killing your enemy. The commandment not to kill had to be obeyed, but not when it came to survival, and weren't the Jews on the brink of extermination?

These weren't reasons enough for meeting the rebel chief. Torn as he was, Jesus couldn't abandon a family member, yet walking into the jaws of peril was just as bad. Then he spoke the hardest sentence he ever said.

"I am Jesus. This is my brother James. Take us where you want us to go."

JESUS DIDN'T KNOW in advance where they had hidden Judas of Galilee, but when Simon led them high up in the hills, walking narrow paths that could barely be seen in the quavery moonlight, he wasn't surprised. Jews had been rebelling for several generations, and before that the dense hills hid smugglers and their stashes of wine from Crete, dye from Tyre, and any other goods the Romans taxed exorbitantly. As they walked, Jesus could smell the resiny trees. He had sharp enough hearing to detect scurrying feet that froze in alarm as the three men passed by. Sliding scree made the going rough. James kept losing his footing and Jesus had to catch him each time he stumbled.

Simon would look over his shoulder. "All right back there?"

James nodded. To preserve his pride, he didn't ask him to slow the pace down.

Simon's sureness on the path revealed to Jesus that he and James were being led to a permanent sanctuary of the Zealots, not one of their floating refuges. Which meant a cave. The Romans could scout any dwelling erected above ground. Insurrection was serious business, and their web of spies and soldiers was tight. But caves were another matter, being numberless in these hills and below ground.

Jesus wondered if he might have passed such a cave on his wanderings without ever discovering what it was. Two types of people lived in his village of Nazareth, people of the mountains and people of the roads, that is, those who stayed at home and those who traveled. Whoever planted wheat, tended olive trees, or herded sheep spent every waking hour in the hill country. (Travelers who had seen the snowcapped peaks of Lebanon would have scorned the Galilean hills as mountains, but they were heights nonetheless, and cold in winter.) Ever since Adam and Eve had been driven with tears and wailing out of Paradise, survival came from working in the dust. This was demanded by God as atonement. The people of the road were a small minority, men who walked from town to town, seeking whatever jobs they could find. Unless the Romans were building a villa somewhere outside the city of Sepphoris, a massive undertaking that created work for months on end, the traveling *tektons* were lucky to find four hours' labor after a half-day journey.

Jesus heard his father called a *tekton* when he was seven. Joseph had taken him on the road for the first time, and a fat, stumpy trader from Macedonia had used the word when he pointed to a broken wagon wheel, spitting out a curt order before he turned on his heels and walked away. Joseph began patiently to repair the twisted metal wrapped around the wheel shaft.

"That man doesn't like you. Why?" Jesus asked. He'd mistaken *tekton,* which meant "handworker" in Greek, for an insult, the way the Romans threw out *Judacus.* (They couldn't, or wouldn't, say the Hebrew word *Yehudi* properly when speaking to the Jews.) Joseph had his little boy hold the wheel steady.

"You're not going to let that fall and kill us both, are you?" he said.

Jesus grimly shook his head and kept his body stiff until his knees felt like they would buckle. Then Joseph began to do what fathers eternally do once their sons become a certain age. He began to explain the world and their place in it.

"I'm a handworker, and now you are too. We lay stone one day, repair fallen walls, saw wood for beams. The next day we walk to where we are needed, and if we want to eat, we learn to lay a mud floor, build a sheep pen from field rocks, and measure a roof beam. God didn't give us an easy life, but he gave us the whole wide world to see as we walk to the next job."

Jesus listened and nodded. He had watched his patient, brawny-armed father do all those things since before he could remember. Joseph rose before dawn and left the house in his patched tunic and leather apron, returning as late as it took. Every handworker lived this way, and the stories they brought back home with them drew the only picture of the world that Nazarenes knew, except for the stories of Moses and Abraham and his descendants in the Tanach, the holy scriptures.

Since his family were people of the road, Jesus should have been bewildered by the crooked moonlit trails inscribed like writing from the hand of a senile scribe. But Jesus was rare. He was of the mountains and the roads both. James, on the other hand, had never ventured this high. He was panting hard, and his eyes nervously searched the sky for clouds that might cover the moon and throw the woods into pitch-blackness. Jesus heard a night sound, the whisper of bats' wings close overhead.

"There's a sheepfold up ahead, in a big cave," he said.

Without looking back Simon nodded. It was common practice during the grazing months to put up a low stone wall at the mouth of a cave where the sheep could be penned up at night. Jesus had heard their murmuring, the nervous sound of meek animals dreaming of wolves. A moment later, the sheepfold was in sight. The trail led directly to the mouth of a large cave where the embers of a fire glimmered orange in the dark.

Simon gave a quick glance backward warning the two brothers to be quiet. Being used to the mountains, he and Jesus could make their steps quiet at will, moving by stealth over fallen twigs and brush. James lacked this skill, and even though his tread only snapped a small twig here and there, the snap was loud enough to wake a half-sleeping shepherd.

"Hurry," Simon hissed.

If Simon was afraid of the shepherds guarding their flock, then they weren't decoys. Since winter was bringing an end to grazing season, they were wrapped in layers of blankets, insulated from cold and the noise of intruders.

"In here," Simon whispered.

At first there was no "here" to see, but then Jesus saw, through the thick underbrush, a second entrance to the cave. This mouth was barely knee high, a gaping blackness you could barely see against the night's own blackness. He and James got almost flat to the ground, following Simon's lead, and crawled into the opening. They kept crawling along a dirt floor for what seemed like fifty yards, although that was an illusion of the tight space, the darkness, and their raw nerves. In reality the crawl space opened up after twenty feet, and soon they could walk crouched over. This was an excruciating way to go, and Jesus knew that James must be grimacing with pain. But just then they saw torchlight up ahead and heard a new, strange sound—the chanting of prayers.

Prayers in a bandits' cave?

The tunnel opened up, and Jesus saw them, a circle of Jews sitting in a large cave. Heads covered in homespun shawls bobbed back and forth. The figures looked spectral against the dim rush torches whose wavering light made the cave walls shimmer like water.

Simon caught Jesus's questioning look. "It's not the appointed hour," he said. "But there's no law forbidding prayer, not when God is needed. For us, every hour is such a time."

None of the young men looked their way as they approached. James poked Jesus with his elbow, indicating an old man inside the circle. Judas the Zealot—for it had to be him—nodded at his returning son. The father was lean, with the same fierce brows as his son and a hawkish face. He sat on a coarse camel rug and wore no sign of rank. This plainness bespoke the old man's toughness. The fact that he didn't question Simon showed Jesus the rebel chief placed implicit trust in him. And the fact that his son rushed to kneel at Judas's feet indicated that Judas was revered.

"Come," Judas beckoned, and the two brothers drew nearer. James immediately prostrated himself on the stone floor. Jesus remained standing. Judas scrutinized him.

"Why aren't you dead?" he inquired abruptly.

Jesus sensed that the question was a ploy, but he answered it. "Because no one wants to kill me," he said.

Judas grunted. He touched James's head so that he could sit up, then waved the three of them to sit by his side. The circle of young men kept rocking and praying. Judas seemed impatient.

"Your reply is either simpleminded or cunning. I have no time for either. What I want to teach, you must learn quickly or not at all. Is that understood?"

He went on without waiting for a reply. "Why are any of us alive? What has made it possible for the Jews, a wretched people decimated by one conquest after another, to survive?"

"We fight back. We're willing to die," James blurted out.

Judas narrowed his eyes. "Think before you speak. Fighting back is how you get killed when you're outnumbered. Jews have been easy prey for all the generations since Abraham. God richly rewards us for our faith. We should have been exterminated long ago, like locusts burned from a field with torches. But we weren't."

He turned to Jesus. "Give me hope. Can *you* think?"

"Only when necessary," Jesus said.

Judas liked this reply, which was more a parry with light swords than a real answer. "For the Jews," said Judas, "thinking has always been necessary. Now tell me straight, why are you not dead?"

Silently Jesus held his hands together in front of his face, then he opened them, palms up.

Judas burst out laughing. "See?" he cried to Simon. "You shouldn't call them all idiots. This one is clever." Then he turned back to Jesus. "You're right. Your hands show me a book, and that's how we Jews have survived. The Book."

Effortlessly and quickly Judas had seized their attention, something he'd clearly mastered. He fit the part of a rebel leader, skin leathery and tough, eyes fiery when he threw out challenges. His beard was uncut, with a wide streak of gray dividing it in two.

"My brother was also right," Jesus said. "Our people have fought to survive. Not all were killed."

"If the Book has allowed us to survive, what is destroying us now?" asked Judas.

James jumped in. "Straying from the law."

Jesus grabbed James by the collar of his rough wool cloak. "Let's go."

"No! Why?"

Jesus felt Judas's eyes on him, watching to see his next move. The young men in the circle weren't scholars. Each was armed with a knife beneath his prayer shawl, strapped close to the chest. Each was a *kanai,* one who is angry for the sake of God. If Jesus wasn't recruited, they wouldn't hesitate to kill him.

"I know why you brought us here," he said to Judas.

"To teach you," said the Zealot. His tone was no longer fiery, but his hawk eyes didn't waver.

"No, to threaten us. We know where you hide now. We'll have to keep your secret unless we want to be murdered."

A wave of anger crossed Judas's face. The praying circle grew ominously quiet. When Judas failed to recruit a rebel, he often created an adversary. There were no neutral parties in Judea, not now, probably not ever. But Judas hadn't survived this long without being able to read men, and this one wasn't ready to turn against him. He might even be malleable, with the right treatment.

Simon was surprised when his father said nothing, but bowed his head and pulled on his white prayer shawl. There wasn't even a curt nod to dismiss the two brothers. But the son knew that his father must have his reasons, and without being ordered he led Jesus and James out of the cave.

ONCE THE BROTHERS got close to the sheepfold again, Jesus asked James to remove his sandals. His younger brother's soles had been toughened by walking the roads, and he would be quieter going barefoot. The precaution worked at first. The sleeping shepherds, whose fire had gone completely out, could be heard snoring in the thin mountain air. But a few hundred yards later Jesus stiffened.

"That's what I was afraid of," he said.

"What?" asked James, who had heard nothing unusual.

"They're following us."

Jesus gazed at the sky. The moon was still out, but small racing clouds crossed it. He couldn't risk leaving the trail. He saw that James wanted to run, and he held him back.

"Better to wait," he said. Whoever Judas had sent after them knew the terrain too well.

Their pursuers were almost silent and descended on them by surprise not from behind, but from the front—two young men with knives out. Jesus was still holding James's arm and felt the muscles trembling beneath his skin.

The bigger of the two men spoke up. "We're not going to kill you. Show us your weapons, if you have any."

"We don't," Jesus said.

The lead man nodded. "Then stick your arms out. We have to cut you."

Jesus knew why. The rebels wanted to mark them so they could be recognized later. They could also use the marks to betray them to the Romans, in case a hunt began for Zealot sympathizers. "No," he said. "Let us pass."

The two rebels looked at each other. They broke out in a coarse laugh. "It's not a request, boy," the lead one said, even though he was probably only a year or two older than Jesus. "Bare your arm. Now!"

Dark as it was, Jesus could see his brother's eyes widen with fear as the knife blade approached. James broke away from his grip and bolted.

"Get him!" the lead man shouted.

The second one had no trouble catching up with James, who stumbled, almost falling on his face before he'd run a dozen yards. The Zealot leaped on him. There was a brief struggle before the attacker pressed the knife blade at James's throat and swiped it lightly in a crescent curve. It drew a faint line of blood that looked black in the moonlight. James shrieked with pain. He knew that the fatal stroke was coming.

"Stop!"

The attacker looked up. The cry hadn't come from Jesus, but from a voice in the dark. A second's hesitation, and then the figure of a third Zealot emerged from the shadows.

"Who told you to leave the hideout?" he barked. The man was older and taller than the first two, and he seemed to hold authority over them. He glared, and the younger ones instantly lowered their knives.

"Clear out!"

As furtively as they had appeared, the two assassins disappeared back into the woods. Jesus heard a flurry of footsteps, then nothing. By now he was bending over James, who was trembling in shock.

"Don't try to stand yet. Here, hold still." Jesus tore a strip of linen from his long undergarment and wound it around his brother's bleeding throat.

"It's only a line," the third Zealot said, examining the wound with a glance. "They hadn't finished making the sign."

Jesus nodded. The wound could have been caused by a slipped awl or chisel on the job. Once it was healed, it wouldn't give away that contact had been made with the rebels. But James would never forget where it came from. Jesus helped him sit up.

Quietly he said, "If you join them, this is how it will be every day."

It was a hard thing for James to hear at that moment, which was why Jesus said it. He had to break through his brother's illusions about fighting.

Surprisingly, the tall Zealot standing over them agreed. "He's right. Leave it. We'll need fighters next year too, and five years after that." He spoke with the authority of hard experience.

When James was able to stand shakily on his feet, the tall Zealot offered a shoulder to help him. Jesus reluctantly let him lead the way down the trail. The small racing clouds had coalesced into a thick layer, and the moon disappeared. The rebel said little until the lights of Nazareth—no more than guttering candles standing watch in a few windows—came in sight.

"We look bad, don't we? Even worse than you suspected."

Jesus didn't reply. "Just keep one thing in mind," the rebel said. "You have more in common with us than you do with them, no matter how bad we look. Will you think about that?"

"I have my own thoughts," said Jesus laconically. On the way down the mountain he began to wonder if the whole attack hadn't been staged. It would have been an easy way to get them to trust their rescuer, whose voice sounded cunning.

The tall Zealot blocked the trail. He was imposing, even as a silhouette in the dark. With his long unshorn locks, one could have mistaken him for a Philistine warrior returned from the torments of Gehenna.

"What are your thoughts, brother?" he asked Jesus.

"I think Judas is subtle. Perhaps subtle enough to stage an ambush, complete with a rescuer showing up at the last minute."

The Zealot grunted. "You're a rare one, aren't you?"

The night couldn't conceal his surprised look. He didn't argue back. Now they all knew that the "rescuer" was actually a recruiter.

Half an hour later they reached the main road. James had regained some strength and no longer needed propping up. The tall Zealot touched Jesus's shoulder.

"It was Simon's idea. If you come back again, don't trust him too far."

He turned to James. "I meant what I said about needing fighters next year. The fighting is only going to get worse." James hurried away, not looking back.

"I solved your problem," said the Zealot when Jesus hung behind.

"Yes. He won't be tempted again."

"Only evil tempts," the Zealot said. "That's not us."

"Then what do you call what you're doing?" Jesus had already started down the road to catch up with his brother. The Zealot kept pace for a few yards.

"I call it salvation," he said. "Anyway, I'll keep them off you. And if you run into trouble, just give them my name. Everyone knows me. I'm Judas. The other Judas."

Jesus was far enough down the road that he barely heard these words. The other Judas could no longer be made out in the dark, even as a silhouette.

3

GOD ON THE ROOF

Jesus woke up to the most dangerous smell in Nazareth—smoke. He leaped out of bed and ran outside, pulling on his tunic and cloak as he went. This wasn't the warm smell of his mother's bread baking in the hearth. It was acrid and sharp, the smell of disaster.

Jesus saw the curling black trail coming from his roof. He would have cried the alarm, but at that instant he caught sight of a ladder leaning against the wall. He scrambled up, and when his head appeared over the roofline, he saw Isaac, the village blind man squatting beside a small fire of pitch pine that he'd built on the flat mud surface. In one hand Isaac held a knife, in the other a small rabbit trembling with terror.

"No, don't."

Hearing Jesus's voice, the blind man turned his head. "You need a sacrifice," he said firmly. He held up the rabbit. "I had one of my boys snare it this morning." Isaac's wife ministered to him, blind as he was, faithfully, keeping his tunic spotless and his beard long but neat, like a patriarch's.

"What I need is for the house not to burn down," said Jesus as he climbed onto the roof and walked over to the makeshift altar of twigs and sticks.

Nobody knew what afflicted Isaac. He went blind almost overnight, a calamity for his wife and two sons, neither old enough to take to the road. They herded a handful of sheep while their father stayed at home.

When Jesus tried to take the rabbit from Isaac's hands, he resisted. "You've brought trouble to this house. I know where you went, I know who you saw."

Jesus hesitated. A sacrifice was the usual way of dealing with God's displeasure, and since going blind, Isaac had become obsessed with God. In his affliction he had been given a gift, second sight, or so everyone believed.

"No sacrifice for now; just a talk," said Jesus. He sat down beside Isaac, who reluctantly let him have the trembling animal. Jesus kicked the burning sticks and twigs, which scattered and went out. "Maybe God has something else in mind. The Zealots could be right. Maybe we'll perish unless we live by the sword."

"God always has something in mind," said Isaac. "Something mysterious, like choosing a people, but then giving them no power. Who has ever figured that one out?" His voice turned more serious. "Then there's you. You almost have the gift. Almost can be worse than not at all."

Jesus knew that people said this about him, that he was like Isaac, but without the excuse of blindness.

"What do you see?" Isaac asked. "Something has happened. If I can sense it, you must."

Jesus didn't want to answer. He and James had crept in after midnight. Even though the whole family slept in one room, nobody woke up. The two brothers crawled into the pallet they shared, a wool mattress stuffed with straw and laid out on the floor. James, exhausted from fear, fell asleep immediately. Jesus couldn't sleep. He stared at the stars through the one small window that was cut in the wall of the stone house.

The same anxious thought kept racing through his mind. Judas—the other Judas—couldn't protect him. If the Romans wanted to track down rebel sympathizers, nobody could stop them. It was necessary to be quiet and invisible. Easy enough. They had all had plenty of practice at that—centuries.

"Let's go down," he said to Isaac. "We can eat together." His mother hadn't been in the house when the smoke woke him up. She must have gone to the town cistern for water, but Mary would have left behind a breakfast for him of flatbread and crushed olives.

Isaac shook his head. "I'm staying up here. God is here."

Jesus smiled. No matter where he was, the blind man habitually muttered, "God is here." It annoyed people. Jesus was one of the few who took an interest.

"Tell me, rabbi," he said, using the word as a compliment, not a tease. "How is God here?"

Isaac held his hands up. "I feel warmth. There's a glow in the back of my eyes. Isn't that God?"

It would do Jesus no good to protest, as anyone else would, that it wasn't God, but the sun. Isaac would only smile secretly and say, "Yes, and the sun is God, no?"

Jesus watched the last wisp of smoke die out from the scattered altar; he let the rabbit run around the roof, but it quickly disappeared down the ladder. He said, "Why aren't we dead?" The same question Judas of Galilee had asked him in the cave. "Is it the Book?"

Isaac shrugged. "If you stamp on an anthill and pour oil on it to burn it out, you will kill most of the ants. But a few always run away. The Jews are like that."

"You think the Jews are only ants?"

"No, there's a difference. The ones who run away think that God loves them more than the others."

Jesus gave a crooked smile. "It's our curse, isn't it?"

They both knew what he meant. Worrying about God's inscrutable ways was a very subtle curse. A pathetically insignificant people were in love with destiny. To a Jew, nothing could be an accident, anything could be a sign. A sparrow couldn't fall without somebody asking if it was God's will.

But Jesus's attention had wandered. In his anxiety over the house burning down, he'd overlooked something. He had woken up alone. Even if his mother had gone to the cistern and his father had gone to find work, where were his younger brothers and sisters?

"Come," he said. "We've got to find my family." There was no need to lead Isaac by the hand. He could clamber down a ladder faster than Jesus.

"I should have told you," said Isaac. "Everbody's run away."

"Why didn't someone wake me up?" Jesus asked anxiously. The whole village would run away only if garrisoned Roman soldiers were marching into Nazareth. Urchins on the road served as lookouts, racing ahead to warn the village that the great beast, the Roman army, was lumbering its way on its hundred feet.

"Everyone was in a panic. I was sent back to fetch you," said Isaac.

"So why didn't you?"

"No time to talk. We have to get to the woods."

Jesus took Isaac's hand and led him over the rough ground as fast as the blind man could run. He didn't blame Isaac for getting distracted. God did that to people who had the gift.

They wouldn't get far if the Romans were anywhere nearby. But Jesus knew of a secret place, a hollow under fallen trees. The villagers, who only went into the woods for fuel or escape, wondered why Jesus went there to wander. It was simply added to the list of his strange behaviors.

The hollow was large enough to conceal them both, and they had reached it just in time. The house of Joseph stood on the edge of Nazareth. They could see it from their hiding place, and now Roman soldiers in cadres of four and five were scattering out from the center of town. They carried torches.

"How many people will they take?" Isaac whispered. From the short distance he could hear the crackle of the torches.

"It depends on how scared they want us to be," Jesus said grimly.

The soldiers tossed a torch into a house not far from Joseph's. Even though the walls were made of fieldstone held together with mud plaster, it went up quickly once some oily rags were tossed inside. The straw beds caught fire first and lit the low wooden beams overhead.

Jesus felt sick. But the Romans wouldn't destroy the whole town—they needed the taxes. Burning down a few houses would send enough fear through the people. This was low-grade retaliation for the meeting in the granary the night before. The next step would involve dragging someone away to be tortured. But that was the limit. If rebel sentiment flared up again, the Romans would come back, this time by night when everyone was asleep. A few would survive the fire, but the Romans were used to that. A few ants always managed to escape.

JESUS DIDN'T HEAR the screams of the man who died. He was Hezekiah, old and crippled, an enfeebled patriarch. His family didn't want to leave him behind, even in a panic, but he insisted on taking his chances. The Romans wouldn't care about one old man. That day only three houses had been burned to the ground. As Providence would have it, Hezekiah's was the first. A charred body was pulled from the ashes and wrapped in a winding sheet. From a distance the wailing of women reached Jesus's ears. It was a time for everyone to gather in mourning, but he used it to get away. He had a secret ritual to perform.

Without being noticed, he walked to the *mikvah,* the ritual bathing place outside town. A natural spring was located there, and generations ago a cistern had been dug around it. The Torah demanded that impurity be washed away, but not in a tub or sink filled by hand. Only fresh running water fulfilled the law.

Jesus approached warily. If a woman was inside the mikvah taking her monthly bath, it would be trouble. This was almost entirely a woman's place, and men stayed away. The mystery of a woman's cycle was not for the righteous to observe or think about. But all the women would be at the funeral, so he was safe for a few hours.

Steps carved into the natural rock led down to a small chamber shaped like a box, just large enough for one bather. Jesus stripped off his tunic and wrapped a cloth around his waist. The water was at his feet, deep and clear. Even in the dry season the bath was always full.

Jesus had brought a small clay vessel of pure olive oil. He dabbed it on his forehead and stepped into the water, which came up to his waist. It was bracing cold in the winter, and he submerged himself quickly. He came up with a gasp and spoke his prayer out loud.

"God, forgive my transgression. Show me my sin and lift it from me."

Jesus saw a shadow before he saw the man who cast it. As he whirled around, the intruder said, "I can do a lot more for you than he can. I can save you."

Jesus scowled. "I don't want your kind of salvation."

The intruder was Judas, the tall Zealot. He stood on the platform where Jesus had dropped his clothes, and in the cramped chamber there was no room for two people—he had trapped Jesus in the water.

"Don't worry. I'm not going to shout for anybody. I know why you're here, and it's not because you think you're a woman."

Judas's voice was low and calm. He sat down on the platform on top of the fallen tunic and cloak, making the point that Jesus was going nowhere. He said, "You're going to have to shiver a while longer until we finish our talk."

Without waiting for a reply, Judas continued. "I've had you looked at. Everyone says you're strange. But we both know that." Judas smiled and waved a hand. Any man caught in a mikvah was strange. Or holy. He narrowed his eyes.

"First things first. The world isn't coming to an end. Do you believe me? Or are you as crazy as people say?"

"I believe I'm freezing. Go away. It's because of you and your meeting that an innocent man died."

"You're lying," Judas said coolly. "If you thought it was us, why are you here making atonement? You think that somehow you're to blame, isn't it? That because of your sin the soldiers invaded. I'd call that megalomania." Suddenly Judas grinned. "We need more of that."

"Enough. Stand aside." Jesus had gotten over his embarrassment at being discovered and was getting angry. It wasn't unlawful for him to be at the mikvah. Everyone, men and women, bathed in the pools around the Temple in Jerusalem before entering the sacred place.

He tried to step up onto the platform, but Judas pushed him back. "So what are we going to do about your sins? Are you one of those weird jobs who are so guilty that the world must end, all because of them? Answer."

The two glared at each other. The water was cold; Judas stood his ground. Jesus was not going to get out unless he answered.

"No, I don't believe the world's coming to an end. The people who believe that are desperate. They can't see any other way out."

"I can."

With a swift gesture Judas pulled a curved knife from his sash. In the confined space it was no more than a foot from Jesus's naked body. He backed away, but Judas leaned forward, extending the knife.

"Here's your escape. Isn't that what you want?"

He turned the blade around and offered the handle to Jesus. Jesus shook his head, remembering the sword that Simon had waved in the granary. This was the same cheap trick.

"Take it," Judas insisted. "You'll be a different man. Has God done anything for you? You think you want forgiveness, but you're lying to yourself. You want strength, because you're sick and tired of being the lamb. What good are lambs except to lie on the altar and have their throats cut?"

Jesus's heart raced at the sight of the weapon, and not just because Judas might stick it in him. Without knowing why, he held out his hand and grabbed the knife handle. Judas nodded, barely smiling.

"Hold it. Feel it. I'm not asking you to be an executioner. I'm asking you to take your power back. What right did anyone have to steal it from you?"

Abruptly the Zealot cut himself off; he turned and ran back up the steps. Jesus felt his muscles relax. He climbed out of the water and put on his clothes, the whole time still clutching the knife. When he emerged from the mikvah, Judas was standing in the sun by the entrance.

Jesus said, "Take it back. I don't want the power to kill."

Judas shook his head. "What kind do you want? The power to be killed? Well, congratulations. You have plenty of that."

Jesus felt his face turn red. When he held the knife out, Judas knocked it to the ground with a swipe of his hand. "Pick it up when you're ready to be a free man. Or leave it there to rust. That's what a slave would do."

Judas didn't wait to see what effect his scorn was having. He had already turned on his heels and started down the rocky path. Jesus watched as his visitor suddenly broke off to the left and disappeared into the shadow of the pines. A moment later he was gone from sight.

Hezekiah's corpse had been taken to the house of the dead. It was too low and too small to accommodate the entire village, and as Jesus approached the ones gathered outside, mostly younger boys, turned their heads—but only for a second. They were used to Jesus, whose wandering habits had earned him a nickname, "the stray."

He stopped and kept apart. On the roof some men were praying, Isaac among them. Their bodies swayed, and the air was smudged with the ash they rubbed in their faces. Isaac, however, had his sightless eyes open and his face turned upward.

As part of his gift, Isaac could see the angel of death when he approached. "A glorious thing, with clattering wings and a falcon's head," he told him. "He shrieks like a hawk too, to attract the soul to God. Dying souls are afraid and need to be shown the way."

The blind man and "the stray" had conversations like this when they were alone. Now Isaac's face began to glow; he threw his arms into the air. He saw what he saw, the one angel the Jews could count on when the others seemed to desert them. Jesus half believed that he saw him too. The air shimmered over the house of the dead, but not from summer heat this time of year. It would settle everything if he could be as certain as Isaac, but Jesus might only be imagining.

What he wasn't imagining was the knife whose weight he felt in the palm of his hand. He had had enough of being a slave, and if Judas knew where the road to freedom led, the choice was clear. Jesus knew he could never kill, but as the Zealot said, being killed was a skill the Jews had mastered all too well.

4

THE FIRST MIRACLE

On the way to Jerusalem the two travelers talked about miracles. "Would you like to become a *magus?*" Judas asked, using the term that the Romans applied to a wonder-worker.

Jesus looked baffled. "Why?"

"It's going to take one to lead the Jews," Judas said. "When everything else fails, try miracles. The first miracle is to get people to believe in your powers."

"I don't have powers," Jesus said.

"You don't actually have to possess them. Is it a miracle when bread rises? It is if you've never seen it before."

They had been on the road for three days and were only a day away from the capital. Judas was overbearing and full of ambitious plans. He ordered Jesus to stand guard while he slept, sometimes all night. He spent hours ignoring his young follower—that was the only way he saw Jesus—planning what would happen when they reached Jerusalem. Then, as Galilee receded behind them, Judas became more relaxed. The threat of capture was much lower in the south, where the spy system of the Romans was still weak.

"There's something weird about you," Judas said. "You could already pass as a magus. I've heard talk."

Jesus fixed his eyes on the ground. "What do they say?"

They were passing on foot through a stretch of desert with only parched underbrush all around. Judas pointed up ahead to a lone thorn tree. "Let's rest."

The tree's shade was thin and hot, but the travelers welcomed it. A goatskin water bottle was passed between them while Judas related a story told behind Jesus's back. Mary, his mother, saved figs over the winter in a jar to hand out in springtime at Passover. The village children loved her for it, but one year when Mary opened the jar, green mold had gotten inside. The figs were ruined, except for two on the top.

"They say you found your mother crying, and you told her to invite the village children anyway," said Judas. He eyed Jesus sharply. "Is any of this true?" he asked.

Jesus was smiling faintly. "So far."

"When the children came, you were seated by the door. In your lap was a basket covered with a napkin. You reached under the napkin and pulled out a fig for each child. They were delighted, and you never ran out of fruit. But anyone allowed to peek under the napkin would have always seen only two figs, no matter how many had already been taken."

"That's true," Jesus admitted.

"So the tale of a miracle began to spread," Judas said. He narrowed his eyes. "You've never heard this?"

"I was twelve," Jesus said mildly. "Twelve-year-olds have imaginations."

"What does that mean?"

Jesus hesitated. He knew he was about to fuel a streak of deception in Judas. Then he explained. "At that age I sat and dreamed all the time, and one thing I dreamed about was the wonders performed in the time of Moses. I asked myself why I, and everyone else I knew, had never seen any miracles. My mother had pulled out her jar of figs for Passover week, as usual."

"And they weren't rotten," said Judas, knowing full well where the story was going.

"I spread the rumor that they were," Jesus said. "When my mother invited everyone, people were confused, but they came anyway. It's not hard to fit a basket with a false bottom. I kept two figs on top and reached under for the rest."

Judas burst out laughing. "You cheated! I knew you were a magus. I just didn't know that you discovered it so young."

"Does it please you that I cheated?" Jesus asked. "I felt important for a few days, but my mother found out about the rumor of moldy figs. She didn't scold me. The look in her eyes was my punishment."

Judas was not pleased anymore. He poked at the sandy ground under the thorn tree, lost in thought. When they got back on the road, he scowled for a while before saying, "Just remember, we still need a wonder-worker. The Jews are slaves, and slaves don't have a clue how to free themselves. The best they can manage is an uprising, and those are doomed before they begin."

They took turns riding the donkey that Judas had procured for the long journey. He'd given Jesus a new pair of flimsy sandals, warning him, "Save these for the city. We have to blend in, and your road shoes are a dead giveaway that you walk the road." He ordered Jesus to clip his beard short so he wouldn't look like a bear who'd escaped from the hills.

On the very edge of Jerusalem, the stone-paved highway was packed, a traveling bedlam of traders, pilgrims, beggars, and handworkers seeking God and fortune in the capital. Jesus saw his first monkey, an Arabian horse, and pygmy goats no higher than his knee. He saw travelers decorated with earrings, neck rings, nose rings, and more exotic baubles. For every gold fillip, there was a bandit by the side of the road keeping an eye out to snatch it. When Jesus went to sleep at night rolled in a blanket, there were sounds of drunken laughter and piercing screams. He marveled to think that Rome must be ten times as madcap.

"I know what I'd call a miracle," said Judas. "If we survive this mission."

"Will we?" Jesus asked.

It was the first Judas had spoken about any mission or its dangers. Even now he kept it cloaked in mystery, saying, "Don't worry. It's taken care of." When the gates of the city appeared in the distance, Jesus gaped. It had been years since his parents took him to the ancient home of the faith. He had fantasized as a young boy that the gates would be solid cedar, so massive that the wood's perfume could be smelled half a mile away, and even farther away a pilgrim would see glints of light flashing from their gilded surface.

Judas shook him out of his reverie. "You need to know everything," he said, and unfolded their mission in an undertone as they rested by the roadside.

Simon the Zealot was sending them on a lethal mission, to stab the high priest of the Temple. It was time, he said, to aim terror at the heart of the collaborators, not low-ranked rabbis, but the Sanhedrin, the high court itself. Judas told Jesus about going back to the rebels' hideout a few days after confronting him in the mikvah. Sitting on the cave floor, he listened silently as he was given his orders.

"The Sanhedrin convenes in the Temple every day to hear cases. There are twenty-three judges on ordinary days, but don't worry about them. Focus on the high priest and chief judge," said Simon. "Cut off the head and the whole beast will die."

Judas paused. He saw Jesus's body stiffen. Like any provincial, he was in awe of the Temple and had hardly dared to step within a hundred feet of the priest caste. Striking the high priest would be no different from striking at God.

"You consider the whole court traitors?" Jesus asked quietly.

"They are the only ones who can put the king on trial, and what is Herod but a whore of Rome?" Judas said. "Yet the Sandedrin does nothing."

"Is that the same as betraying God?" Jesus asked.

"What do you mean?"

"When we met, Simon said that the Book must be upheld, which means obeying the laws of God. Isn't that what these priests and judges do?"

"You're not looking at them right." Judas was growing impatient. "Collaborating with the enemy is a crime against God."

"What choice do they have?" Jesus said. "Priests are the most visible among the Jews. If they don't cooperate, they will be killed. I've made you angry, but I have to understand. A priest may bow to the Romans outwardly, but love God in his heart. All of us do the same thing. What makes us less guilty?"

Judas could hardly contain his anger, but he let Jesus continue.

"I came with you because something has to be done about the suffering in the land. But if I find that you aren't righteous, helping you would only add to that suffering. How am I wrong?"

Although he seemed on the verge of erupting, Judas spoke in a low, even tone. "You can't betray the mission. I vouched for you. This is your test. I'm the only thing that stands between you and what the Zealots will do if we fail."

"My test is murder?" asked Jesus.

"Listen to me. If we succeed without being arrested, even Simon and his father will trust us. We become lieutenants and then captains."

Jesus was stunned. He had lied and prepared in secret to leave Nazareth. His family could be told nothing, for fear that the Romans would torture them if he were captured. His furtive movements were noticed, but then there was a piece of luck. The family of Hezekiah, the old man burned in the fire, wanted to offer a sacrifice at the Temple. His wife was old and enfeebled; the sons couldn't leave their scrawny flock. Jesus stepped forward and offered to make the journey for them. His benevolence was greeted with tears; the old woman fell to the floor and embraced his feet.

Stifling his guilt, Jesus tied a clutch of coins into a small pouch around his waist—even though they were mostly copper, these represented half his savings. He somehow calmed his mother's fears and his brother James's suspicions. On the last night he slept fitfully, and getting up at dawn, he jumped when his mother said, "Where's Judas?"

She meant the youngest son in the family of Joseph, who was five. The only sister who was within earshot, Salome, ran to fetch the boy. Jesus forced himself to eat breakfast, sunk in gloom. Mary asked no questions; their eyes didn't meet. Then the family crowded in the doorway to watch Jesus leave; he could feel their eyes on his back until he was out of sight. He had no chance to say good-bye to his father, who had left early to find work, or his other brothers, Joses and Simon, who no longer lived at home.

Now he turned to Judas. "I can't become a murderer, not even to save our people."

Judas gave him a crooked smile. "You won't murder anyone. That's the beauty of it."

Jesus felt the color rise in his cheeks. "What are you talking about?" he demanded.

"Calm down." Judas reached into his sack, pulling out bread and olives and a scrap of dried lamb. "Eat. This is the last of the provisions," he said coolly.

Jesus knocked the food out of his hands and jumped to his feet. "I trusted you!" he shouted. "You tempted me with freedom, and now you lead me to sin?"

He was amused at Jesus's consternation. "What are you now, a rabbi?" he said dryly. "It's not for you to say that an eye for an eye isn't just."

"Then you be the rabbi. Tell me what is just."

"No, I don't aim that high. Just trust me one more day. You trusted me to save you from the Zealots once before. I can do it twice."

Judas examined the bread that Jesus had knocked into the dust. Judas sniffed at it and threw it away. "Now we'll go hungry." He got to his feet. "I told you we won't be killing anybody. We'll just appear to. Are you coming?"

Judas picked a bramble switch to use on the donkey. Jesus watched him, wondering if he could still run away. But they both knew he couldn't. Judas couldn't protect him if they abandoned the mission.

"All right," Jesus said reluctantly. "What now?"

Judas mounted the donkey and kicked it into motion. "We're going to perform the first miracle, the one that gets people to believe in our powers."

THE TEMPLE WAS bewildering and huge, a city within a city. Its walls enclosed the only perfect safety the Jews had ever known. When they congregated there, the outside world disappeared. In its place had been built a promise of God's glory come to earth. Gleaming white walls dazzled the eye; shaded colonnades provided peace and shelter. The inner sanctum, the Holy of Holies, was the smallest part, but the richest, because there the devout faced God.

Surrounding the Temple court was a vast stone colonnade. Jesus and Judas merged into the crowd, which clustered around money changers and sellers of offerings. Few were rich enough to sacrifice the sheep and bulls required by sacred law. All they could afford was a minor offering of cereal grains or turtledoves.

Jesus eyed the birds hanging in wicker cages. Feeling the pouch of coins tied around his waist, he asked how much a single dove would cost. The seller eyed him disdainfully. "I don't cheat the customer," he said sourly before even naming a price. "If you want a bird for free, go back to the farm."

Judas pulled at Jesus's arm, impatient to move on. The colonnade enclosed a vast courtyard where thousands of people could stand. Jesus had always seen it jammed with worshipers shoulder to shoulder. For poor people like his family, the law demanded one visit a year to offer sacrifice on Passover, but Joseph couldn't always manage to bring them all. Being the oldest son, Jesus had come three times, James once.

The first time, when he was thirteen, he saw Paradise. The smells were intoxicating, the air heavy with cedar and myrrh. He asked his father why there were no lush plantings of the kind that once adorned the Temple of Solomon, not even a tree.

"It was left barren to symbolize the desert that the Jews had to cross to reach the land that God would give them," Joseph said. "Or maybe it stands for grief."

There was a lot to grieve over. Inside the innermost and most sacred place stood a single gold, oil-burning lamp, replacing the dazzling array of gold that once filled the Temple of Solomon. Then unspeakable calamity fell. The Temple of Solomon was razed by Babylonian invaders. To crush the spirit of the Jews, everything sacred was smashed or looted. There was no Ark of the Covenant anymore, no scrap of the manna that God had miraculously sent when his children wandered for forty years in the wilderness with Moses. Meager as they were, the Jews were decimated, the remnants dragged into captivity in Babylon. When they were finally allowed to go home, the trek to Jerusalem lasted for months. But the first thing every Jew who survived the trek did was to join in the rebuilding of the Temple.

It was hard to forget their sacrifices, even though they took place five hundred years earlier. The holy site made Jesus feel less and less enthusiasm for the rebel conspiracy, while for Judas the same sights aroused contempt. He kicked aside a boy who was desperately trying to hold back two sheep that his father had brought for sacrifice. The animals had panicked and were trying to bolt. The ground was littered with sheep and cow dung.

"What kind of people are we? Look at them. They step in filth to get to the altar. That's their path of purification," Judas said with scorn. He took Jesus by the arm; it was time to reconnoiter.

The judgment hall where the Sanhedrin sat was a separate structure that faced into the great courtyard, but it had another entrance on the outside facing the city. This was to signify that the court was sanctioned by religion and yet also held civil authority.

"Or maybe it's a warning that the judges are two-faced," Judas said. Judas did his scouting swiftly, moving his sharp gaze around every corner of the site. He took Jesus to the city entrance, to make sure it offered an easy escape. He was disappointed. The entrance was small and packed with angry petitioners pushing and shoving to get inside.

Judas asked nothing of Jesus and said nothing to him. The time was early morning, before the judges had arrived, so the inner chamber, the actual seat of judgment, was deserted. The crowd jostling at the door would be twice as large once court was in session. Judas decided not to wait.

"But we haven't seen how many guards there will be," said Jesus.

Judas seemed unconcerned. "Guards are for arresting people. They won't be interested in us unless we commit a crime."

Jesus had showed patience, allowing his companion to preserve an air of mystery around his plans, but no longer. He stopped on the Temple steps and demanded an explanation.

"There are some crimes that only look like crimes," said Judas cryptically. He held out his hand. "Here, give me your money."

"Why?"

"Just hand it over. What happened to trust?"

Jesus backed away, pressing his hand over the hidden pouch of coins. Every move Judas had made up to this point wasn't a test of trust, but of power. Judas sensed that he had finally gone too far. "I'll tell you everything, but you can't back out. Agreed?" he said.

Jesus shrugged instead of agreeing, but Judas was satisfied. "We aren't going to stab anybody. We're going to be magi and make it all look real. Nobody will have a reason to arrest us, but the Zealots will think we've succeeded. It's a brilliant plan, really, if I have to say so."

His sly smile didn't reassure Jesus. Judas ignored his doubting expression. "We're going to take your coins and buy a cage of turtledoves. Then I'll drag you into the court shouting that you stole it from me. We'll make a ruckus and charge right up to the judges."

"They won't let us get that far," Jesus protested.

"We'll be moving too fast for anybody to react. By the time the guards take a run at us, we'll be close enough."

"For what?"

"For this." Judas's smile deepened as he pulled out a small glass vial filled with a greenish yellow syrup. "It's poison. I'll smear it on a thorn, and once I get close enough to a judge, I'll scratch his arm. That's all it takes."

Jesus was alarmed. "So you're going to kill one of them after all?"

"With a prick? Of course not. But it's a fast poison, and he'll go into fits almost immediately. In the meantime, I'll put on a show. The guards will be on top of me. As they drag me away, I'll go crazy. I'll wave my arms and curse the judge, bringing down God's wrath. At that moment the poison will make him seize and thrash about. If we're lucky, he'll keel over and pass out."

If not a brilliant plan, it was an impressive one to Jesus. Everyone's eyes would be transfixed by the show of a magus's curse working before their very eyes. The priest would recover in a matter of minutes, saving them from prison. They might even walk away if Judas talked fast enough.

But Jesus had his doubts. "Simon will find out that we didn't kill anybody."

"So what? I'll say we stabbed a priest, but missed a vital area, in all the uproar. Nobody will be able to contradict me."

"But I thought you wanted to kill one," said Jesus.

"Don't be simple. I'm using the Zealots. That's why I need you. You're like me. You can see how idiotic their schemes are. It's only a matter of time before the Romans wipe out every last one of them. You think an empire survives if it tolerates rebellion?"

Jesus was wary. If Judas was using the Zealots, he was just as likely to be using him. "Why should I do what you say?" he demanded.

"Because when you said you wanted to see the suffering in the land end, you meant it. Not like most of those bastards. They've been rotting in caves since before either of us were born, and when they come out, the Romans pick them off. Besides, no matter how many collaborators the rebels knife in the back, do you see anyone's life improving?"

It was a powerful question, to which Jesus had no good answer.

• • •

JUDAS PLANNED THEIR staged miracle for the next morning. They spent the night wrapped in their cloaks under a viaduct. It was a filthy, stinking place, and as soon as he was sure that Judas had fallen asleep, Jesus got up to wander the streets. The air was freezing, and at any moment a bandit could jump out of the shadows, but he had to think. One small thing that Judas had said stuck in Jesus's mind: *You're like me.*

Was he? In every side alley he passed, Jesus saw heaps of dirty rags with people sleeping under them like moles in their burrows. Open sewage ran in the gutters. Suddenly a cough made him turn around. A boy with his feet wrapped in burlap had sneaked up behind him in the dark. The boy was too frightened of strangers to speak up, but he held out a bony hand as small as a stray dog's paw.

"I'm sorry," Jesus mumbled.

"Just a scrap, master." The boy's bulging eyes and the parchment skin over his face said that he was starving. It had taken him a moment to understand the dialect of Aramaic that Jesus spoke in.

"I'm not your master," Jesus said gently, thinking to himself, *I could be in your place. I don't know why I'm not.*

Instead of walking away, the boy grew angry. "You're lying. You came here with food. They all do."

Jesus was about to say, "I ate it all," which was the simple truth. At that moment it seemed like a sin. He crouched down to the boy's level. "Where's your family? Do you have a name?" The boy shrugged and looked away.

Suddenly Jesus was startled. In the darkness, the beggar boy's profile looked exactly like that of his younger brother,

Joses, one of the two who had left home. Jesus reached into his tunic, bringing out the smallest copper coin in the pouch hidden there. It wasn't his money to give away, but he handed it to the boy.

What he got back wasn't gratitude. The boy shoved him hard, taking advantage of Jesus's crouching position. He was thrown off balance, and instantly the boy was on top of him, scrabbling with his clawed hands for the rest of the jingling coins.

"Get off me!" Jesus cried. The boy was fierce, gasping and grunting like an animal as he scratched at Jesus's skin.

The boy had no chance against a man, and once Jesus recovered from his surprise, the boy had to flee. This he did, quickly and silently, on his ragged feet. Jesus didn't run after him. It took a moment before he wanted to get up, because he was overwhelmed with a welling sorrow. The sorrow of self-betrayal.

Jesus had secretly made a pact with himself when he was barely older than this beggar boy. Nothing fascinated him but God, yet he promised himself that he would live and work like everyone else, because that was a duty imposed by God. One day, as the law prescribed, he would marry and raise children. But being in the world didn't mean he'd have to be of the world. Like Isaac the blind, Jesus could look where no one else could, toward the divine place. Where that place was he had no idea, which involved another promise. He wouldn't accept tales of God's kingdom, a magical realm above the clouds furnished with a throne of blazing white marble, whiter than the kind the richest Roman could afford to line his lavatorium with.

Jesus had no right to question scripture. He couldn't even read and write properly other than signing his name in Hebrew and Latin letters, making out the alphabet, and piecing words together syllable by syllable. But the scriptural scheme was too neat—starve in this world so that God can usher you into a palace when you die. In that regard he felt the same as Judas. Jesus could see why people suffered even when they themselves didn't. They suffered from hopeless fantasies about God's love, when all he showed them, if you were brutally honest, was indifference and contempt.

Jesus wiped away a streak of blood on his side where the street urchin had scratched him and wearily got to his feet. Being in the world but not of it wasn't working. He shed too many tears for someone who should be detached. Judas had a plan to get people to pay attention, and if it took a false miracle to carry it out, that was better than no plan at all.

5

THE HOLY WOMAN

Early in the morning, when the city's shutters were still closed, Judas and Jesus made their way to the Temple and bought a cage of doves under the colonnade. Judas haggled and got a good enough price from the Syrian merchant that there were a few coins left over, which they spent on bread. It was a paltry breakfast, hardly enough to calm the gnawing in Jesus's stomach. They ate squatting on the street outside the Temple gates. Jesus kept quiet and after a while handed half his bread to Judas.

Judas took it without thanks. "You're not going through with this, are you?"

Jesus shook his head.

"Why not? Because you think it's ridiculous? Great events begin this way, by attracting attention. People can be played. They want to be played on, believe me."

Jesus didn't meet Judas's gaze. "It's wrong to do it in the Temple," he murmured.

Judas guffawed. "In God's house, you mean? My little trick won't bother him. Look at what he's already allowing. Ten times worse than anything I could dream up."

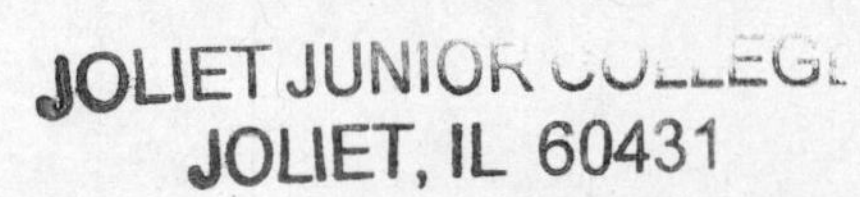

"Still."

"You found a convenient moment to be pious, didn't you?" Judas turned, mocking, raising his hands in imitation of a village rabbi on Shabbat. "Hear me, God. I'll do anything to save your people, except risk my hide. There are limits, don't you know?" He took the small chunk of the bread Jesus had given him and threw it into the street.

Jesus jumped to his feet. "I'm going."

"We both are," Judas replied, his voice cold and hard. "The holy city hasn't revealed all its charms yet." He collared Jesus and began to drag him away. "Don't fight me," said Judas grimly as Jesus struggled to pull out of his grip. "I'm going to show you what you really are, a hypocrite. The same as the rest of them."

When he felt Jesus relent, Judas let him go. They walked together down a narrow street feeding into the Temple grounds. Both were angry, but Judas knew that his younger companion doubted himself. He'd have to use that doubt to conquer Jesus's fear.

"Look over there," he said, halting halfway down the street. He nodded toward a stall where a petty merchant sold head cloths and cheap relics. "You see his three daughters behind him? They're not his daughters. They're holy women. That's what they're called."

Without looking to see if Jesus followed, Judas walked up to the stall. He greeted the seller of relics, a burly man who stood with his arms crossed over his chest. He asked him what was on offer.

"Whatever you please. The goods aren't hiding. Take a look."

The seller gave a curt nod. Behind him three veiled women who were crouching in the shadows stood up. They looked like ordinary women except for the gold ankle bracelets revealed by skirts an inch too short. One after another, each parted her veil, giving Judas a flashing peek at her face. Their skin was pale; kohl had been applied heavily around the eyes to make them seductively black against the paleness.

"Age?" Judas asked.

"The youngest is twelve, the middle one fifteen, and the oldest sixteen." The seller, making no disguise of his real profession, gave an oily smile.

"Liar. The oldest one barely showed herself for two seconds. She's twenty if she's a day," Judas said. "A hag." He glanced over his shoulder. Jesus was hanging back several yards, averting his eyes.

The procurer winked. "Your friend is shy. Tell him there's nothing to worry about. All my holy women are pure. The twelve-year-old is a virgin."

Judas had heard enough. "Maybe later. Tell your virgin to go to the priests to be worshiped. If she's a virgin, it must be a miracle."

The procurer didn't take offense. He laughed as one man of the world would with another. With a wave of his hand the three women sank silently back down into the shadows.

When he returned to where Jesus was standing, Judas looked satisfied. "Good, you're shocked. Now let's get on with it."

Judas was canny enough to leave his companion to his own thoughts. Jesus would soon realize on his own that he couldn't do without Judas. The Zealots would seek revenge if he disavowed them, and if he retreated into his usual dream world—for Judas had little doubt that there was a streak of religious delusion at work here—Jesus couldn't deny the danger he'd brought to his family.

At this point, it was only necessary to put Jesus's trust to a small test. When they got to the Temple gates, Judas handed Jesus the cage of doves. "Go inside. Make the sacrifice you promised. I'll meet you in the judgment hall in an hour." Without another word Judas turned on his heels and walked away, disappearing into the crowds that were swelling as the day grew on.

Jesus watched him go and wished that he could run in the opposite direction. But Judas's assumptions were right. Jesus had been sunk in doubts all morning. He realized that he was powerless; without Judas he had no protection. Cradling the cage of doves in his arm, he joined the stream of devotees making their way across the vast sun-bleached courtyard to make their offerings before the sanctuary. This was a smaller building at the back of the Temple grounds, each stone hewn as the scriptures demanded, without the use of iron tools. Stone could only be hacked with stone. Faced with such slow and painful labor, the ancient builders could be excused for leaving the blocks rough-sided, but they were doing holy work and the walls of the sanctuary were smooth enough to gleam in the light.

By contrast the inner chamber was rough and as smothering as a cave. Jesus stopped for a moment and let the crowd jostle past him. None could trespass into the priests' area, but all had been told of what the sacred place held. The Ark of the Covenant was lost, but the descendants of Abraham and Moses had done everything they could to recreate the First Temple. The high altar, the flickering menorah, the showbread sacrifices were all placed before God.

Once, when he was twelve, Jesus had been so entranced by these sights that he couldn't bear to leave them. His family was staying at an inn over Passover. It was time to leave, but Jesus had slipped away saying that he wanted to catch a ride in one of the wagons at the end of the long train that had come from Nazareth. When no one was looking, he ran back to the Temple, which was by that time deserted. He had the place all to himself until two old priests tried to shoo him out. To linger longer, the boy began to ask questions. If God gave Moses the tablets to last forever, how could he allow the Gentiles to steal them? Why did the Persian king give a thousand workers to rebuild the Temple—did God come to him in a vision?

His first questions were childish, but after a while Jesus began to trust the old priests, who were flattered at having their knowledge tested. He opened up about the dilemmas that had been bothering him a long time. If a Jewish baby was stolen or abandoned, like Moses floating in a woven basket down the Nile, would God still know that it was Jewish, no matter where it was taken? If a man was so poor that he couldn't afford to travel to the Temple to make sacrifice, could he atone in his heart instead and earn God's forgiveness?

The priests were taken aback and asked the boy how such complicated questions came into his head. Because he knew people whose children were stolen, Jesus said. And others so poor that they couldn't afford so much as a handful of barley flour for the altar. The priests were touched and grew expansive. One discussion led to another; the strangely wise boy was allowed to eat with them and sleep on a pallet beside them. By the time Joseph retraced the road and returned to the Temple, panicked and angry, Jesus hardly realized that three days had passed.

Reaching inside the cage, Jesus pulled out a dove, the whitest one of four. It went completely still in his hands, trembling with fear. Jesus joined the line of worshipers waiting to approach near the sanctuary. As they inched forward, he saw a priest come out, a huge man wearing a thick leather apron over his robes. A bloody knife stuck out of his belt.

The priest shouted at a man in front of the door who was tugging at a calf; the animal was so terrified that it was bawling and struggling to slip out of the noose around its neck.

"Move it in or get out!" the priest shouted. The smell of blood that he gave off made the calf more terrified. Impatiently the priest drew his knife and swiped it across the calf's throat. The cut was just deep enough to nick an artery without slicing through it. Blood began running down the calf's chest; it staggered, barely able to stand.

"There," the priest said, holding out one hand. The calf's owner groped for some coins to put in it; with his other hand the priest held the calf, ready to drag it inside. It had quit bawling and was easy to subdue. The other worshipers farther back in line stopped grumbling about the delay.

The smell of blood reached as far back in line as where Jesus stood. It was an old, remembered smell. He had seen the altar before, with animal innards burning amid acrid smoke and choice bits of meat sliced off the carcass to be set aside for the priests. Sacrifice had never sickened him before. Now he stepped out of line and held the dove high over his head.

He let go of the dove, but instead of flying upward, it fluttered to the ground. Fear had weakened the creature so much it couldn't fly. The sight made several men laugh—some hick had been fooled into buying a sick bird not fit for sacrifice. Jesus knelt down and lifted the dove again, but he didn't throw it into the air. The dove had quit moving or even trembling and died in his hands.

No one took any notice this time. Something else had caught everyone's attention. An old woman was trying to push her way in line. She was small and wizened. Her hands fumbled with some flowers she had picked along the way, and her shawl had fallen down around her shoulders. Apparently she didn't notice that her head was uncovered. Some men began pushing to get her out of the way; others called her an old whore, expressing their outrage at this defilement of the Temple.

"Let me help you, mother. Are those flowers your offering?"

The old woman squinted up at Jesus. For a moment he was afraid that she might be out of her wits and would scream at him. Women weren't allowed in line, and flowers weren't acceptable offerings. But her agitation, which had been increasing, suddenly calmed. She blinked like an owl caught in daylight and muttered, "Draw near me, I will run after thee. The king hath brought me into his chambers."

"What?" said Jesus, taken aback.

"Don't they teach you anything?" The old woman shook her head haughtily. She shut her eyes, as if drawing words from a deep well of memory. "We will be glad and rejoice in thee; we will remember thy love more than wine." She smiled to herself. "Could anything be more beautiful?"

The line was moving forward again, trying to shove both of them aside. "If you dragged that crone out of her cave, take her back," one man jeered.

"Here, mother, come with me." Jesus gently pulled the old woman by the sleeve while covering her head with her shawl. She was paying no attention to the disturbance around her.

One bony hand clutched her flowers tightly, and yet she didn't totter. When the other hand reached out to hold on to Jesus, her grip was firm. They made their way to a stone bench by the cisterns where all the women went to purify themselves before worship.

"The Song of Songs," she said. The old woman tilted her head quizzically. "That's what I was quoting. Didn't you recognize it?" Jesus shook his head, and she sighed. "They tore down Solomon's Temple, but they can't kill his words." She gave a knowing tap to her forehead. "Now you know my secret. Don't tell anybody."

Jesus smiled. Even if she was half cracked, the old woman made him forget the trouble he was being pulled into. "And what secret is that?" he asked.

She bent toward him and whispered, "I'm a sinner. I can read. They'd tear me apart if they knew."

Jesus couldn't hide his surprise. "Who taught you?"

"My father. He was rich, but he had no sons. It sent him into such despair that he brought tutors to our house at night. I learned to read by candlelight, like a conspirator in a cave."

This last part was accompanied by a sharp look, much sharper than anything an addled crone would deliver. Before Jesus could react, she said, "God doesn't need help picking out the wicked."

"Because there are so many?" asked Jesus.

She shook her head. "Because the covenant isn't in there." She nodded toward the huge oak doors of the sanctuary. "God knows the righteous by reading their hearts. Out of the whole world he picked Noah, didn't he? Out of riotous Sodom he picked Lot. The righteous shine by their own light. He'll pick someone else soon."

Jesus looked down at the old woman's hands, which were at work plaiting together her flowers, mostly small pink roses of the kind that grew wild in ditches around the city.

"Is it enough to be righteous?" he asked quietly.

"It has to be. The wicked will always win by numbers, won't they? No matter how many lambs are born in the spring, there will always be more wolves to eat them."

The old woman, musing to herself, remembered another line of scripture. "I am the rose of Sharon, and the lily of the valleys. As the lily among brambles, so is my love among the daughters of Zion."

She had finished her circlet of roses, and without warning she placed it on Jesus's head. It was too small and tilted at an angle. She giggled, and as often happens with old people, her giggle made her sound like a child again. "How pretty that looks on you. Like a crown."

WHEN THE TWENTY-THREE judges filed into the hall, Judas bowed with the rest of the petitioners. The members of the Sanhedrin were men of stature, all the more so because of their tall black headdresses and the gold clasps that held their robes closed. Authority didn't enrage Judas the way it did the Zealots. What made a man a judge over other men? Not God, of that Judas was certain.

As a boy in Jerusalem, he knew his father's friend Simeon, who lacked the cunning to make money. Everyone pitied him and his wife, who lost two babies because her milk was too thin to nurse them. People whispered behind her back of a curse, but Judas's father took his son aside and explained reality to him.

"She's half starved and probably poisoned. Simeon creeps off when no one is looking and buys rancid flour with weevils in it and God knows what else. Ground bones, marble dust. They can't afford anything else."

As Simeon's plight grew worse, he started to love the Torah more. He became obsessed with figuring out what God wanted, because it must have been God's will that separated a wretch like Simeon from a rich neighbor like Judas's father. In the third book of Torah, Leviticus, more than six hundred laws were handed down to guide a righteous life. Simeon went half blind studying them every waking hour—Judas could smell the tallow from candles burning next door after midnight.

Even though Judas was a boy and Simeon a man, he pitied him. God's laws were a tangled mare's nest; only a fool would be so deluded that he'd attempt to unravel them. Then, by some miracle, the same Simeon who "accidentally" dropped by their house when soup was on the table gained a reputation for wisdom. Poor people who couldn't afford to consult a priest came to his house. He parsed the law for them and settled the most baffling queries. If a Jew buys a horse without knowing that a Roman once owned it, is the horse defiled? If a Jew eats pork that has been maliciously put into his food without his knowledge, how great is the sin?

After a time, the meager offerings enabled Simeon's wife to nurse her next baby in good health. One day she appeared in a new head covering without holes in it. The neighbors couldn't believe this change of fortune, but Jews worship learning even more than God (so his father told him), all the more if they have no learning themselves.

Now there he was, Simeon the judge marching into the hall with the rest of the Sanhedrin. He had become someone Judas must bow to. Judas imagined, as Simeon took his seat, that their eyes met for an instant over the throng. Did he sense the truth, that he was the one Judas had chosen to poison with the thorn?

"I'm here."

Judas had been so absorbed that he didn't see Jesus by his side. He had the cage of doves in his hands. "Are you ready to play your part?" he asked.

"God willing," Jesus replied.

It wasn't the right answer, but it would have to do. The first plaintiffs were approaching the long judges' table, gesticulating in the air as they wailed their complaints. Judas pulled Jesus by the arm and shoved through the crowd, crying out for justice as he waved the caged birds over his head.

"Help me, sirs. I've been cheated! My sacrifice is defiled!"

Judas wailed like a peasant, bowing obsequiously to the judges, who were still yards away. The packed throng didn't want to let him through, but Judas was louder and more persistent than anyone else. He rolled his eyes alarmingly; foam gathered at the corners of his mouth.

"See, see?" he cried. "They sold me filthy birds, full of disease. My child is covered with sores just from touching them!"

People shrank back in horror. The Temple guards were too far away to reach Judas in time. He drew within earshot of the judges. They were indifferent, however. With bored faces they nibbled at dried figs and olives while waving their hands over petty cases decided by the hundreds every day.

Lagging behind, Jesus saw that Judas's prediction of events had been astute. He forced himself so close that the judges had to notice him. Judas furtively plucked the poisoned thorn from his robe and pricked Simeon's neck. The judge, who was whispering to a colleague and doing his best not to notice the rank odor of the crowd, barely felt the prick. But the guard stationed behind him saw Judas's quick motion.

"Hey!" he cried, making a lunge over Simeon's shoulder to grab Judas's collar. At a signal, other guards rushed the table. Judas allowed himself to be taken, shoving Jesus back so that he might escape notice. He loudly cursed as he was being dragged away.

"Hypocrites! God would never do this to an innocent man!"

Simeon shrugged and tossed a bowl of olives on the floor—stale. The milling bystanders were jostled; a few laughed, most pushed harder to fill in the gap left when Judas lost his place.

Judas waited until he could see Simeon's neck swell, the flesh turning a livid purplish red. He cried, "I will exact vengeance, O Israel!"

Judas's timing was perfect. Simeon's tongue lolled out. He made a strangled sound, like someone crying out as a garotte squeezed his throat, and fell to the floor, seizing violently. The crowd was stunned.

But then calamity. Another man, his face cowled in a black hood, pressed forward. Before anyone could grab him, he bent over the fallen judge. For half a moment he could have been mistaken for a mysterious healer sent out of nowhere, until someone screamed, "A knife!"

The cowled figure held the blade in midair so that it could make its full effect, then he plunged it into Simeon's chest. A fountain of blood gushed upward, drenching the assassin's robe. He slipped in blood as he stood up, almost losing his balance, yet everything had happened so fast that no one seized him. The killer shouted a few incomprehensible words (later a scribe claimed that it was a prophecy from Isaiah, "He will smite the nations and slay the wicked").

At last a spectator was able to pull back the assassin's cowl, and what it revealed made Judas go white.

"It's them," he cried. "Run!"

Judas didn't glance at Jesus, but if he had, he would have seen a face as pale as his own. They both recognized one of the young Zealots from the cave. The rebels hadn't trusted Judas after all, sending a spy to watch him and to complete his mission if he failed.

Because Judas's sham miracle had come so close to the stabbing, the crowd pounced on him. Cries of "traitor" and "blasphemer" arose. But Judas had realized the danger so fast that he and Jesus were almost at the doors before they were seized. Judas threw off the two old men who jumped him.

"Go, go!" he screamed.

Another man, much stronger than the two old ones, had grabbed Jesus, who only escaped by slipping out of his cloak.

They were lucky enough to run out the doors that faced the street rather than the inner courtyard. A mob of Jews would have trapped them on the Temple grounds. Judas paused to rip off telltale marks—amulets, headband, earrings, Temple cap—that would give them away. Jesus hesitated to do the same.

"What is it? Don't be a fool," Judas shouted. He grabbed the thin chain around Jesus's neck. It broke, and a silver mezuzah fell to the ground. Jesus bent to pick it up, but Judas screamed that there was no time and pulled him away.

They had wasted precious seconds. A pack of Temple guards had tumbled into the street. They spotted the fugitives and began to shout for the crowd to stop them. But nobody obeyed; some lounging Roman soldiers began laughing and baying like hounds chasing a deer.

Judas dragged Jesus into a narrow alley crammed with vendors' carts, which would slow down their pursuers, but he hadn't counted on the gate at the end of the alley being locked. Judas struggled desperately with the rusty iron latch.

He ordered Jesus to help. Instead of pounding on the gate or shouting for help, however, Jesus stood aside without a word.

"What's your idea? That God wants us to get killed?" Judas accused him angrily.

At that moment a nearby door opened, and a woman appeared. It would seem impossible that she'd do anything but scream and run back inside. The Temple soldiers were at the mouth of the alley, pointing at the fugitives and screaming obscenities at the fruit vendors who wouldn't get out of their way.

The woman took all of this in. Instead of retreating, she pointed inside her house. What choice did they have? Judas and Jesus took refuge; she slammed the door behind them and bolted it.

"It will take them a couple of minutes to break in," she said. Her voice was remarkably composed. "I think we can make it."

We? There was no time to question her. Judas nodded, and the woman quickly led them through a series of rooms leading to an outer passage. It was dark and almost too narrow for a grown man to squeeze through. After a few yards the passage turned a corner, and they were thrown into total darkness. A smuggler's route, Judas surmised.

Whether that or something else, the passage was devious. Just before it broke out into the street—they could already spy sunlight at the far end—a hidden door disguised to look like part of the plastered wall opened off to the left. The woman pushed, and the door swung open on creaky hinges.

They made it through just in time, crowding into a cramped, suffocating closet. Judas's nerves tingled; he heard the clumping boots of the guards running past them down the passageway, the iron nails on their soles clanging against the stone floor before they faded away and he heard nothing.

"Just a few seconds more," the woman whispered. "Sometimes they're cunning."

Sure enough, a second set of boots ran past the door. Their pursuers had split up in case they met with a ruse. After a minute these faded too, and there was silence again Cautiously the woman opened the door, peering both ways.

Jesus grabbed her hands to mumble his thanks, but she pulled away. "I don't need thanks. I need to come with you."

"Why?" he asked.

Yet Judas already knew, because he hadn't averted his eyes when the "holy women" unveiled their faces that morning. This one was the oldest of the prostitutes, the one whose procurer claimed was sixteen but was obviously older.

"All right, you can come," Judas agreed. Once they were safe, he could find out why she had decided to trust them. That a prostitute would want to run away from her procurer was obvious. Anyway, she knew the dizzy, winding warren of the Jerusalem slums better than any Temple guard would have.

The nameless "holy woman" didn't move immediately. She looked steadily at Jesus. "And you?" she asked. "Can you stand it, traveling with a whore?"

He gave a nod, which was enough. She led them back the way they had come, then out through the dead-end alley. She produced a key for the locked gate, and two minutes later they were a long way from the Temple grounds.

Judas's nerves stopped tingling, and the buzz of excitement died in his ears. The three of them were walking slowly in a straight line down a dark lane lined with animal pens. Goats and sheep milled together listlessly, ignoring them as they passed. Judas looked back at Jesus, who was last in line. He had said nothing along the way and had acted indifferent to the whore after he realized who she was. Judas was a little mystified, wondering if this was the passivity of a perfect follower or the inscrutability of a potential betrayer.

Jesus wasn't being enigmatic. He kept seeing the silver capsule of the mezuzah Judas had ripped from his neck. He had been desolate at its loss. The Book demanded as a *mitzvah,* a commandment, that every righteous household have a mezuzah nailed to the doorpost at the threshold. But a new custom had arisen among the workers who traveled the roads. They wanted to carry Yahweh's protection with them wherever they went. Now Jesus had thrown it away.

Judas would have scorned this superstition, and Jesus never mentioned it afterward. Who deserved God's protection? A judge was lying in a pool of his own blood. The Zealots knew that they had two renegades in their midst and would hunt them down. For some reason, none of this threatened Jesus. It was as if he could see inside the mezuzah where a tiny prayer was inscribed on a scrap of parchment. Trailing after the "holy woman" in the dust of the street, he repeated the opening words to himself: "Hear, O Israel, the Lord your God, the Lord is One."

There was no other comfort to be had.

6

WILDERNESS AND WORSHIP

The three fugitives decided to run toward the Dead Sea. At first Judas refused to head south. He painted a grim picture of barren shores and sun-parched villages. "What do you expect to live on, salt? The farmers pray to avoid famine every year."

Besides, he argued, the Romans were in firm control of the area. They recruited spies from the desperately poor. "There's no rebel underground there. Nobody's going to hide us. If we go north where we came from, we'll find sympathizers."

"And Zealots who want to kill us," Jesus reminded him.

"They don't know anything yet," said Judas. "Maybe their assassin didn't make it back. He could be rotting in Pilate's dungeons for all we know."

The three runaways were sitting around a low campfire in a gully full of brush that couldn't be seen from the main road. Jerusalem was now a day's walk behind them, and God had been kind. None of the Roman patrols gave the three nameless travelers a second glance.

The holy woman had disclosed that her name was Mary, the same as Jesus's mother. So far she had taken no part in the argument. A woman wouldn't expect to. Instead, she had gathered twigs for the fire, brewed a bitter tea from wild herbs in a pot she found discarded by the side of the road, and listened silently.

Suddenly Mary spoke up. "Galilee is too dangerous. Informants will be thicker where there's rebellion. The fewer inhabitants, the better." The two men stared at her, but instead of shrinking back, Mary lifted her head. "I'm not invisible, and I have a brain," she said. "Remember who got you out of the city."

Judas flared up. "You say you have a brain. How much of a brain did it take to be a whore?"

"Enough to earn this." Mary patted her robe, and the sound of jingling coins could be heard.

Judas jumped to his feet. "You have money? Why are we starving out here like animals? We can find an inn. Give it here."

Mary refused. "I'm saving it for a desperate moment. When we have to pay for our lives. Which do you prefer, a night in a good bed or getting out of jail?"

Judas retreated into sullen silence. They all knew she was right. One day, perhaps very soon, a corrupt jailer might need to be paid off. The point was to postpone that moment as long as possible.

They slept in the gully that night, maintaining their small fire screened by underbrush. Since Mary had found a spot far away from the two men, Judas argued to Jesus again for heading north to Galilee. Jesus wouldn't listen. Since Mary had money and served them by taking on most of the work, the group shouldn't split up, however disgruntled Judas acted.

"All right, have it your way," said Judas. "Guard the camp. I'll sleep."

It was easier to comply than to keep arguing. Doing without a lookout was too dangerous. The terrain encircling the Dead Sea was mostly wilderness, which held a natural attraction for anyone who needed to hide: robbers, escapees from Roman jails, tax evaders, and the like.

They continued their course to the southeast for several days.

Every night brought the necessity of finding a place to bed down. Two men and a single woman walking into a village aroused immediate suspicion. Mary went to market to buy their food. She knew how to be frugal. Three people could be sustained for a shekel on fish scraps and day-old bread. Scowling vendors shoved the goods at her, then shooed her away so as not to taint their stalls. They didn't know Mary's profession, but her brazen haggling, the seductive traces of black kohl around her eyes, and her direct gaze gave something away.

"Let them stare," she said. "Last week it was my business to attract stares."

Mary had desperately wanted to escape Jerusalem and degradation. But she wasn't the same country girl who first came there. Her hands were smooth from unguents and aloe cream. She wore toe rings and a tiny gold hoop in one ear. It had been necessary to advertise. You never knew when a casual glance from a man on the streets might lead to a seduction. Because she was tall but fair-skinned, almost milky, passing glances were common, and Mary had to steel herself from the contempt of other women and the leers of men.

"All the other merchants sell their goods," she said. "In my trade, I am the goods."

Before Jesus agreed to travel with her beyond the walls of Jerusalem, he made Mary promise that she wouldn't offer herself anymore. Judas grumbled that just walking by her side was a sin. If they were living by the Book, the two men shouldn't even eat the same food as she did or let her cook their meals.

Mary laughed. "You'd rather go hungry than break the law? Look around. Not many Pharisees are wandering the roads to catch you."

She kept up a brave front, but Mary was worried about being abandoned by the two men. One night when they were alone, she confided to Jesus. "Judas can't decide whether to treat me like a woman or a leper. At least if I were a leper, he wouldn't be so tempted to touch me."

Seeing the shocked look on Jesus's face, she softly said, "You're the only one I can put some hope in. You can tell the difference between the sinner and the sin."

Jesus protested. "I've joined with Judas. We're only strong together."

Mary gave him a knowing smile. "Don't be tough. It doesn't come naturally to you."

Without warning she took his hand and held it tight enough so that Jesus couldn't draw back. "What makes this different from your mother's hand or your sister's? A touch is a touch, until somebody makes you afraid by naming it a sin."

Jesus was thoroughly embarrassed by now, and Mary let go. "See? You didn't lash out at me. That means you're in doubt."

"What's good about that?"

She stood up. "There's more to life than the Book. You're young. You'll find out soon enough." It was a condescending thing to say, and she walked away to wash her face in a nearby stream without explaining herself. But that night Jesus awoke under the stars with a start. Mary was crouched beside him, touching his arm.

"Here," she whispered. She thrust her money bag into Jesus's hands. "Keep it safe, and give it back when I ask for it. Don't tell him."

"Why do you trust me?" Jesus asked.

"I'm not sure. Maybe I'm trapped with two thieves." She left Jesus to work things out on his own.

A few days later, Jesus confronted Mary. "You were forced into being with men. You're not really a . . ."

Mary shook her head. "No. Things happened."

Her story was violent and short. When Mary was of age she was betrothed to a young apprentice in the gold trade. He was absorbed in his work, bent over a table for hours making intricate braided necklaces and religious ornaments. One day, just before their marriage was to take place, the Romans burst into the shop and accused the gold workers of counterfeiting imperial coins. The owners of the shop had two choices. Turn over the guilty party or have every worker carted off to prison. Jonas, her betrothed, the youngest of the apprentices, was sacrificed.

"He didn't go away bravely," said Mary. "He went away in tears. The way you might have."

She said this almost as if it were something to admire.

With Jonas condemned as a traitor, Mary became too dangerous for anyone to be seen with. She ran away to Jerusalem one night, leaving behind her dowry, so that her younger sister would have a chance to marry.

"I was alone, but it wasn't long before a panderer spotted me and kidnapped me off the streets. He beat me for a while, then put me to work. Nobody whores who isn't a slave. That was six months ago. I've watched and waited to make my escape." Mary looked at Jesus curiously. "How did you figure it out?"

"I looked past what you wanted me to see."

Mary was lost for a reply.

"What are you two gabbing about?" Judas said irritably, just returning from scavenging the terrain. Fish scraps and moldy bread turned his stomach after a few days. But he had managed to find a dripping honeycomb that came with the price of the stings all over his face. They were already starting to swell. In his sleeve he had wrapped some withered crab apples. Judas crouched on the ground and divided his find.

"We were talking about you," said Mary, meeting Judas's annoyed glance. "You've been wanting to abandon me, but you haven't found the right moment to break it to the boy."

Before Jesus could protest, she said to him, "Don't you know that he thinks of you that way? As his boy?"

"Enough!" Judas shouted. He had long, brawny arms, and without moving from the spot where he was crouching, he reached out, slapping the woman hard enough to knock her over. Mary cried out and lay still, not moving.

Jesus bent down and picked up her portion of the honeycomb, which had fallen in the dust. He tried to clean off its sticky surface with his fingers. "Here," he said quietly, handing it back to her. "I'm not worth starving over."

He turned to Judas, still speaking mildly. "Remind me, what makes you more respectable than she is? You scheme in caves with criminals. You got an innocent man killed in a holy place. Maybe you're the one who should be ashamed before God."

Judas stiffened. "You have no right. I do it all for God."

"So you get to name what is your sin and what isn't?" Jesus didn't wait for a reply. "If you have that right, so does she."

Judas snorted with contempt. "A whore without sin? Thank you, rabbi, for the lesson."

They ate in silence, and soon it was time to move again. Bushwhacking seemed safer than chancing the roads and bandits. They began hacking their way through thorny underbrush, following the course of a rocky streambed starved for water.

When Judas pulled out of earshot, Jesus said. "He won't bother you from now on."

"Why? He didn't believe you back there," said Mary. "You can see how his mind works. If I'm guilty, that lessens his sin."

"He's afraid of me now," said Jesus.

Mary looked skeptical. "I've never seen a lamb drive away a wolf. I've been carrying rocks under my shift in case I have to defend you."

Jesus smiled confidently. "I know him now. He's the kind who finds it unbearable not to be followed. My threat is that I can walk away."

There was a long way to go before they had any hope of a friendly roof over their heads. All three of them were hiding their faces from God. For the moment there was nothing to separate them from murderers, Samaritans, and the desperate of the earth.

SOON THEY GAVE up bushwhacking for narrow side roads. At camp Judas still handed out orders as if he were commanding a band of fifty rebels instead of two exhausted wanderers. At nightfall he would hand Jesus his knife to cut down pine boughs for their makeshift bedding. When Jesus came back with an armload, Judas critically examined every branch, throwing half of them away with disgust. Likewise, he'd spit out water that Mary brought to him, complaining it was too foul to drink. Most of the time Judas was too distracted to notice either of them. He ate his food staring at the ground and answered direct questions with only a "hmm," after which he got up and walked away.

Behind his back Mary laughed at him. "You know what he's doing, don't you? He's making big plans. In his mind you and I are stepping-stones to his greatness." She thought Judas was delusional.

Jesus was past looking for omens, yet one crossed his path. It happened on the fourth day away from Jerusalem. As they were traveling along a deep ravine, he looked up. Overhead was a large rock that looked like the profile of an old man. Jesus shook his head, but not because the rock was so curiously real in the way it depicted the old man's nose and beard. He had seen the same outcropping two days before—they had wandered in a circle.

"Look," he said. "The Moses rock."

Mary's eyes followed where he was pointing. "Is that what you call it?" She frowned and her voice rose. "I've seen that rock before."

Judas, who as always had taken the lead on the trail, looked over his shoulder. He'd become used to the way Jesus and Mary talked together in low voices. Mary shot him an accusing glance, but Jesus pressed her shoulder, and she kept quiet. She had lost all trust in Judas, and she was impatient, simply biding her time.

"We'll leave whenever you decide to," she said in a fierce whisper. "But don't wait so long that you find me gone."

As a Jew, Jesus knew that God's plans were a secret (like Judas's, he thought with a smile), and when his people wandered in the desert for forty years, what saved them? Scripture said that manna was given to sustain them, but Jesus realized that the lost ones weren't living on bread, even divine bread. They lived on the vision of Moses. What looked aimless to the outward eye he knew was part of a hidden design. The chosen people weren't lost in a desert; they were lost in a puzzle. Only to the worthy did God reveal the key to the puzzle. Which meant that Judas wasn't delusional at all. He was trying to figure out God's hidden purpose. Would he be able to? Jesus had no way of knowing, but when he saw the curious rock a second time, it hit him. God would allow them to be lost until they stopped being blind. That was their test.

No one discussed the reality that they were walking in circles. All three of them just quietly walked the entire day. The next day was Friday and their first Shabbat on the road. The still waters of the Dead Sea looked like lead under a sullen sky. As daylight dimmed, they sat down by the side of the road. The law forbade them to travel after sunset. All at once a wind came from the north, a howling, vindictive wind that drove them to seek shelter.

"Come on!" Judas shouted. Pelting rain had soaked them through after barely a minute. He pointed to the dim outline of a small structure in the distance. They wound up huddling in a farmer's lean-to as darkness descended.

Mary produced the last of the food. She also brought out a candle. "You decide about this," she said, turning to Jesus.

Shabbat always began with the woman of the house, mother or daughter, lighting two candles, or one if the family was very poor. Jesus hesitated for a moment, then he nodded. Mary set the candle upright on the ground. She didn't wait for Judas's rebuke. "Turn away if you have to. We are commanded," she said.

Mary struck the flint that she had brought with her from home. But the wind was seeping through cracks in the shed, making it hard to strike a flame. For several minutes Judas watched her efforts with undisguised disdain. "Let me," he growled, but when he reached out for the flint, Jesus pulled his hand back.

"Tell me first. Why do we do this?" he said.

Judas was irritated. "Let's just get on with it, rabbi. We're miserable, but at least we can pray."

Jesus shook his head. "Why?"

"Why what? Why a candle, why Shabbat? You're being ridiculous. This is what our people do."

"Shabbat was supposed to remind our people that we are holy."

Judas was about to throw Jesus's holiness back at him when a strong gust suddenly blew open the rickety door of the shed. It thwacked Judas in the back and dashed cold rain on his already soaked robes. This only infuriated Judas further.

"Stop preaching at me!" he shouted. He kicked the candle out of Mary's hands and slammed the door shut again. "We're not inside the law anymore. You and this"—he didn't dare to say *whore* again—"you're living in a dream. Wake up, and do it quick, or we're all going to wind up dead."

"It's not given to know the hour of our death," Jesus said. "Shabbat is our true life. We stop everything to remember that we will never be outside the covenant." He said this hesitantly. It troubled him to remind Judas of the most basic things.

Judas's voice took on an edge of hysteria. "One good swipe from a Roman sword, and your head will be outside the covenant. How many candles are going to save you, rabbi?"

"God is going to save us," Jesus said firmly.

"Why, because no one else cares spit about us? Let me tell you, they don't."

"Because I'm going to give him a reason to, starting now."

Without backing down, Judas let it go. He watched glumly as Jesus crawled on his hands and knees, scrabbling in the dark to find the lost candle. When he did, Mary wiped off the dirty wick and went back to striking her flint. A spark caught fire, and a moment later she was praying. *Blessed are you, Lord, our God, ruler of the universe, who has sanctified us with his commandments and commanded us to light the lights of Shabbat. Amen.*

Out of caution she mumbled the words to herself. Jesus knelt beside her. He expected to hear Judas storm out, but when he opened his eyes, Judas was slumped in the corner, his head between his hands.

"Ruach Adonai," Jesus murmured, invoking the breath of God that sustains a devout Jew every day. If Judas heard the blessing, he didn't raise his head to receive it. More likely the words were drowned out by the wind that wanted to break in.

Morning began with the sound of wailing women. Their high keening woke Jesus and Judas with a start. Aching from the damp ground and distracted by their soaked robes, they looked around in confusion. Mary was gone. The wailing was clearly emanating from more than one woman.

Mary stepped back inside the dwelling and beckoned with her hand. "There's trouble. You'd better come and see."

Following her, the men saw a large farmer's wagon that had pulled off the road a hundred yards away. A family was on the move; they had ridden out the storm huddled under the wagon. The donkey that pulled it must have panicked during the night, because it had slipped its traces and broken loose.

"What can we do?" Mary asked.

The women were wailing for the beast to come back, but it was barely in sight now, searching out meager grazing as it loped along.

"Nothing," said Judas. "It's their misfortune."

He spoke according to the law. If a Gentile happened to be there, he could hitch the donkey up again without sin. But because they were forbidden to do any work on Shabbat, the two men of the family, who appeared to be father and son, could only stand by and watch.

"I'll go," said Jesus. Mary tried to hold him back, but he was already running across the field. The donkey was old and placid. It let the stranger approach and take the loose bridle. A moment later Jesus led it back.

"It's all right," he said to Mary. He turned to Judas. "I'm listening to your guidance. Didn't you say we were outside the law?"

But the farmer's family took the animal back reluctantly, and one could see that the father was almost angry.

Jesus pointed to a kid goat tethered to the back of the wagon. "Give that one to me. I'll make sacrifice in the next town." The farmer hesitated, exchanging glances with his wife. "And then you'll have the meat to eat," Jesus added. "I promise."

Instead of calming the farmer's suspicions, this seemed to amplify them.

"Your head," the farmer's wife broke the tense silence, pointing at Jesus.

Jesus felt his forehead with his fingers. There was a large welt near the hairline. It hurt to the touch, but he couldn't remember being wounded. "It's nothing," he said.

"I will take care of it. My blessing will atone for your sin," the farmer's wife insisted. Mary and Judas knew that they couldn't cause a commotion and so eventually Jesus was lying in the back of the wagon as the farmer's family set off again. The wife rubbed a poultice on his forehead. It stank, and when she bound his head with a scrap of linen, the pain made Jesus wince.

"Sorry," she murmured and loosened the bandage.

Without asking permission to join the farmer's party, Judas and Mary trailed behind the wagon on foot. They kept a respectful distance, which didn't prevent the father and son from throwing a warning glare at them every few minutes.

Jesus sat up and was surprised to find the world beginning to swim. A veil of black specks, like a swarm of gnats in summer, fell across his eyes. He realized that he was fainting too late to stop it. The swarming specks grew thicker, and he suddenly remembered how he had been hurt. The kind woman at the Temple and the prickly crown of roses she put on him. It had made the tiniest scratch, the last thing that should have caused harm. For a fleeting second he saw the bright pink flowers and heard her giggle—the rest was blackness.

PART TWO

MIRACLE WORKER

7

CATCH AND RELEASE

Jesus awoke to find hands reaching for him. They clutched at his robes, jerking him upright as if they were hoisting a sack of millet. Rain was beating down on his face and angry voices were arguing. Was this part of his fever dream? Jesus tried to ignore the shooting pain in his head.

"You can't just throw him out. Look at him."

"I don't care. He's nothing to us. Come on, boy, pull!"

The farmer and his son almost had the body out of the wagon now. Jesus's sagging weight made the work clumsy. Their sandals kept slipping on the wet floor of the wagon.

Jesus was too weak to protest. His head flopped to one side like a rag doll's. Judas was standing beside the farmer's wagon in the road, his face livid.

"The sin will be on your heads. Is that what you want?" Judas shouted.

"We're done carrying him. He's all yours now." The father's voice was hard and stubborn. Jesus moaned as his backbone scraped along the wagon's splintered floorboards. He had been surrounded by the fog of pain for so long that it didn't matter anymore. What Jesus feared was blacking out again and descending into a void worse than any physical torment. In this gaping darkness, he saw sharp-fanged demons gnawing at his heart and dragging him further into the darkness.

The wound on his forehead stank; his flesh was suppurating. He could faintly remember Mary peeling away the bandage. A greenish ooze rolled down his forehead, and Mary turned away so that Jesus would not see her weep. The rain felt cool, and he wasn't shivering despite being exposed to the weather. It was almost pleasant to be thrown away. The pain would end. He wouldn't have to dwell on how he had failed his God.

"Wait. I said wait, dammit! We can pay."

Jesus was barely conscious enough to hear the words. This time it was a woman's voice, Mary's. He felt fingers fumbling at his waist. There was a jingle of coins, and then the rough hands lowered him to the ground.

"This ain't much."

"It's what you're getting. Who are the Gentiles to rob us when Jews can do the work?"

Mary was haggling again but this time over him instead of a fish head.

In the midst of the shouting, Jesus saw a glimmer of golden light. It was faint and far away, but moving closer. As much as he had despaired, the sight made him glad. Jesus was afraid to wake up in Gehenna, the hell reserved for those who died outside God. A place where eternity was measured by the creeping pace of agony. The golden light flickered, and there was a voice in his ear.

"Keep still. Don't say a word."

It was Judas, and the glimmer was nothing more than the quavering oil lamp he held in his hand. Jesus groaned.

"Did you hear me? Not a sound."

What was happening? Jesus tried to move his head. He was lying on the floor in a stuffy room. There were straw pallets scattered on the plank floor and Jesus realized that he was in a shabby way station used by the poorest workmen for shelter when they were on the road. One man nearby was sleeping under a dirty blanket. Everyone else was awake, silently crouched, staring at the door.

When he realized that Mary wasn't there, Jesus groaned again. He had to find her. He grabbed Judas's arm, which Judas mistook for an attempt to speak. He held Jesus's jaw shut with his hand and whispered fiercely, "Romans. They're just outside. If you want to stay alive, pretend to be asleep."

But there was no time for pretending. The door burst open, and two legionaries came in, stamping mud off their boots. Behind them trailed a small, nervous man in tall black Jewish headdress. One of the soldiers pointed in Jesus's direction.

"Is that him?"

The nervous little man nodded, then scurried away.

"All right, you lot. On your feet. Now!" The legionary who was in charge barked out orders.

Weakly Jesus rose with Judas supporting almost all of his weight. He kept his eyes on the ground as the Romans approached, but they headed past him. The lesser soldier kicked the sleeping man under the blanket, who didn't stir. The soldier cursed at him. Still the body didn't move.

"Came to ground like a dog," the soldier muttered. He knelt and gingerly pulled the blanket back. The man's face was flecked with angry red spots; he had been dead a while.

The soldier leaped to his feet. "Look at him, sergeant. We haven't heard about no plague."

"Do I look like a frigging doctor? Whatever it is, we're all in the soup now." The sergeant swept the room with his sword. "Out, all of you. You're being quarantined, and no bellyaching. I'll warrant you've seen the inside of a jail before."

A grumbling procession trickled out into the alley. Judas pulled Jesus as far away from their captors as he could.

"Where is she?" Jesus could no longer hold his question.

"Gone."

Jesus's heart sank. Judas had no more to say, and seconds later they were forced back into step with the soldiers. The small bedraggled group then joined up with a larger Roman squad on the main street of the small town consisting of a row of tumble-down mud dwellings and stalls lining the highway. Mary's coins had bought them passage to this place before the farmer finally dumped them.

Shame had brought Jesus to this place. The shame of a captive people had closed around him like a noose and made him the same as everyone else. He had tried to fight for the Jews, which meant for God. The result was ashes, the same that his forebears had rubbed on their faces, swaying back and forth as they wailed their misfortunes. Jesus felt a stab of pain. He looked down and saw that both ankles were raw and red, surrounded by circular wounds.

A second stab, this time much stronger, forced a groan. And then he saw the image of a fox kit trapped in a snare his brother James had set. The trap was laid for rabbits, but the kit was small enough to get caught in it. When Jesus and James approached to free it, the kit snarled and snapped its jaws. Overnight he had been chewing on the snared leg, turning the skin and fur to pulp. Now in panic the creature tried to run, and the leg bone split with a crack. A second later the kit was gone, leaving a trail of blood and half a leg wrapped in the noose. The two boys were sickened.

"At least it can run home," James said hopefully. But Jesus knew that the kit would bleed to death on the way.

He took no hope from this memory. Sin was the noose; the kit was himself. What good had he done except to gnaw at his wound? Eventually he and Judas would be killed, dragging Mary with them. There had to be another way.

Jesus hung his head and waited until it was his turn to be marched to a makeshift jail on the edge of town. The prisoners were summarily thrown into a cramped holding cell.

"Hey, we'll suffocate in here like this," somebody shouted.

The departing sergeant shrugged. "It won't be crowded once a few of you drop dead." The soldiers were bored and ready for their daily ration of dried lamb and red wine fortified with brandy to keep it from spoiling.

Judas stared at the cell's small window high and out of reach. He then rolled himself up in his robes, leaned against the other huddled bodies, and closed his eyes. "Sorry, boy," he muttered.

The bracing cold had initially revived Jesus, but the reprieve was temporary. He felt feverish again and could stay on his feet only so long before he dropped to the floor. He fought off delirium as he squatted. Existence seemed but a hollow shell. The demons were back and gnawing away the last scrap of his heart. Fighting to stay conscious was only a reflex.

And yet the yawning void didn't claim Jesus. He soon became aware of a man moving deftly around the crowded cell. He could barely make out a man's silhouette as he crouched next to a sleeping prisoner before moving on to the next. A pickpocket wouldn't find much in this place.

The man came closer. Jesus realized he was holding something out to him, a goatskin.

"Water, my son?"

Gratefully Jesus took the offered bottle and drank. "When will they let us out?" he asked, handing it back.

"You can go when you want. The Lord is with you. *Selah.*"

"What?"

The man leaned closer. "We've been watching you."

"We?"

"Yes."

The man remained crouching in front of Jesus, his eyes unseen in the dark but fixed on him.

"They know nothing, they understand nothing. They walk about in darkness; all the foundations of the earth are shaken." The man cocked his head. "But you understand, don't you?"

Jesus was at a loss. Like the old woman at the Temple, the stranger was quoting scripture. The man continued, "I said you are gods, you are sons of the Most High." He leaned close again and repeated the words. "You are gods. It's time to prove it."

Before Jesus could react, the strange man had turned his back and was moving on to the next prisoner, offering water. Jesus reached out to pull him back, and a brilliant flash of light stunned him. It wasn't like the previous flashes of pain he had been experiencing. In fact, the pain was gone, and Jesus felt amazingly strong and alert.

He stood up without weakness in his legs. Or rather he saw himself stand up, because he wasn't willing his body to move. The words the strange man shared seemed to have their own power. Jesus moved without effort. Stepping over Judas, who was curled up in a ball on the dirt floor, Jesus went to the door. The man was right. It was time to prove something.

I am the son of the Most High.

The command came into his head with total certainty. The door, despite appearing locked, had been shut, but never secured. Perhaps the strange man broke in. Jesus pushed and the door swung open. Beyond it were torches fixed to the wall and two soldiers on watch. They had been playing dice on the floor, but had fallen asleep in place with their heads nodding on their chests.

Jesus paused, waiting for more direction. Nothing happened, and his heart skipped a beat. Should he run? Should he shout to wake up the others and lead a jailbreak? Silently he walked around the guards, smelling the sharp stink of liquor on their breath. A second door stood between him and the street. It wasn't locked, and a moment later he was standing out under the stars.

Jesus headed away from town with a steady tread. He felt no impulse to run or to think about where he was going. The region was too poor for cobbled streets, so his footsteps were noiseless in the dust.

After some distance—Jesus had no idea how far—a man came out of the shadows, his face hidden under the hood of his cloak

"Master. Follow me." The man spoke with authority, not in a conspiratorial whisper. He saw Jesus hesitate. "You've been taken out of captivity. I can hide you."

Jesus said, "Who are you? I won't go anywhere until I see your face."

The stranger lowered his hood, exposing a thin, sallow visage circled with a trim beard more like a Roman's than like a Jew's. "Call me Querulus. I'm your friend." When Jesus drew back at hearing a Roman name, the man said, "It's not safe to give you my real name, not yet. One has to be careful. Come."

The two exchanged wary glances, and the man covered his head again and headed down a narrow alley. Jesus followed. There was something persuasive in the stranger's manner.

"Why did you call me 'master'?" Jesus asked as they made their way through passages so narrow they seem to have been made for one shepherd boy at a time.

"I'm an optimist. I prefer to see what might be rather than what is."

Jesus shook his head. "Then you've made a mistake. I will never own slaves or give orders to servants."

"That's not what I meant, master," said Querulus. He chuckled to himself. "I'll stop calling you that if it will make you walk faster."

Clearly the man knew the locale. He strode ahead quickly in the dark, needing no compass or moonlight. Jesus was starting lose the strange feeling of being detached, and the troubling image of Judas sleeping on the jail floor wrapped in filthy rags kept returning. "I have to go back," he said.

"You will see your friends again, both of them. They have served their purpose for now."

The stranger in the hooded cloak grabbed Jesus's arm. They had almost reached their destination, apparently. After a few minutes he pulled open a door leading into a small dwelling identical to the others around it, except that the air inside gave off the warm, spicy scent of sandalwood. Jesus hesitated on the doorstep, and the stranger waited.

"I know that smell," Jesus said.

"Yes, the priests use it in the Temple. Imagine how much it costs to burn something that precious every day. With enough gold, you can turn God into smoke."

Querulus smiled and waited. He had the patience to let Jesus make up his mind whether to enter. The chill of the night air was sharpest now in the hour before dawn. On their trip through the maze of streets Jesus hadn't felt the cold. Now it made him shiver as badly as the fever had.

"You offer refuge, and I accept," he said, "but I can't forget the ones I left behind. You promise to take me back to them?"

Querulus nodded. Jesus gave a troubled sigh and stepped over the threshold quickly, following the warm aroma and the promising fire that was banked in the hearth just beyond.

JESUS WOKE UP after a long, deep sleep to find the sun halfway up in the east. A young woman came into his room and placed a basin of water beside his bed, just as his mother did every morning. Jesus washed his face. He saw in his reflection that the wound on his forehead was gone; when he touched it, there was no scar or tenderness. It might never have existed.

The house was large enough to have several rooms, and the floor was wood, not dirt. Instead of rush torches, the rooms were lit with ornate gilded oil lamps mounted on the wall, and the ceiling had been opened up in the center like a Roman atrium. People of means lived here. Jesus came into the main room, where four people were eating at a table. One of them, Querulus, the aquiline-nosed patrician whose profile could have been engraved on a coin, turned. The group had been conversing normally, like a family rather than rebels. He cut off Jesus's questions with a finger in the air.

"Not yet. Eat with us. Get used to your new life."

Querulus spoke with the same authority as he had the night before. Jesus sat down beside him, accepting a plate of wheat cakes, olives, figs, and dried lamb. He had never had such a breakfast in his whole life. Querulus laughed when he saw how little Jesus took.

"Dig in. Not everyone starves just because they're from Nazareth."

Jesus looked startled. The mention of his village changed the tone in the room, and quickly the other three people at the table, two women and a man, got up and left the room.

"Are they afraid to be seen with me?" asked Jesus.

Querulus shook his head. "Not exactly. But having you under our roof is serious business. Don't stare. I didn't mean dangerous business. This is a safe place."

The way Querulus was acting as host, Jesus assumed that it must be his house. The other man—maybe a brother—was perhaps married to one of the women, while the second woman could be Querulus's wife. Jesus ate in silence pondering these possibilities. He finished the last of his drink, a honeyed wine mixed half with water.

"Why was the prison door opened for me?" Jesus asked.

"A test, a sign, an omen, or no reason at all. You know how Jews think. Haven't you worried such things to death with your blind friend, Isaac?" Jesus raised his eyebrows; Querulus waved away his surprise. "I'm not here to mystify you. Isaac is known to us, and he made you known in turn. Then it was just a matter of finding you."

Jesus gave a wry smile. "What makes me so precious?"

"We'll have to see, won't we?" Querulus got up from the table. "If you feel up to it, I have something to show you."

Jesus nodded. He felt amazingly strong. There was no trace of his fever and no weakness in his limbs. Since being healed was part of the same miracle that freed him from jail, there was no need to draw attention to it. Apparently Querulus and his folk were used to wonders.

The two men left the house. It was almost noon, and the street was busy with activity. Querulus walked quickly, weaving in and out among the donkey carts and peddlers.

"It's a ways yet," he remarked, pointing into the distance. "Ask me your questions, but not all at once. We're going to be together a long time."

At that moment Jesus didn't have any questions. His rescuer acted as self-assured as Judas. This implied that he wanted Jesus as a follower. Yet he had called him "master."

"I want to see my family again," Jesus said. "You know the way to Nazareth. Can you arrange it?"

Querulus shook his head. "Too dangerous. Word has been sent to Isaac this morning. He'll tell your mother that you're safe. Is that all? There has to be more."

They had passed the last house in the small village and were heading across a field of sparse barley and weeds. Jesus thought he heard the faint tinkling of bells up ahead.

"We're getting closer," he said.

"Yes." Querulus looked slightly exasperated. "If you won't ask, I'll have to volunteer. We aren't rebels or fanatics. We are more like observers, but of a special kind. We observe through God's eyes. Do you think that's possible?" When Jesus searched for an answer, Querulus laughed. "Don't fool yourself. You've been trying to do the same thing."

The tinkling of small bells steadily grew louder, and when they came over a small rise, Jesus saw where it came from. A small wedding procession was making its way across the next field. The bride and groom walked under a white canopy held up by four male relatives. The bride's ankle bells rang softly as she went. Querulus nodded toward them.

"We're going where they're going. But it's best if we hang back for now. Discretion."

He didn't explain what they were being discreet about. On second glance, Jesus realized that the wedding procession had no guests, only the betrothed couple and the canopy bearers. Why no guests and no celebration? He would have to wait and see.

They walked another half mile under the noonday sun. The sparse fields gave way to woods; the wedding party plunged into them. They didn't hack their way through underbrush, however. As Jesus could make out once his eyes adjusted to the wooded gloom, a trail had been cleared that was easy to follow. Another quarter mile and Querulus grabbed his arm to hold him back.

"No sound," he said in a low voice. "Creep forward and watch."

The trail had ended without reaching any destination, and the wedding party had vanished. But the tinkling bells weren't hard to follow. After a moment they went silent.

"Look."

Querulus pulled back some thick branches, and Jesus saw a clearing in the woods. The wedding participants were kneeling on the soft flooring of pine needles, only they weren't alone. In front of them stood a boy of about twelve or thirteen, a strange-looking boy in scarlet robes with half a dozen mezuzahs around his neck. His hair reached almost down to his waist and was braided in tight knots.

Before Jesus had time to take in what he saw, the boy gave out a shriek and began to mumble gibberish in a fast, fevered tone. Only it wasn't gibberish, but a garbled prayer that tumbled out of his mouth so fast the words ran together. The bride and groom also started to mumble, their words just as garbled but softer.

The boy started to twirl, his arms flapping, at first slowly, then faster and faster. He kept up the spew of words. As his body whirled, he reached into his robe and pulled out what looked like a black rope. But the rope writhed and tried to crawl up the boy's arm. The bride and groom stopped praying; their eyes widened.

"An adder," Querulus whispered.

The boy showed no fear of the poisonous snake. He thrust his arm in the air as the serpent wound around it. The bride went pale, anticipating what was to come. The boy ended his gyrations. He approached her, the whites of his eyes glistening.

"Lord, put your seed in this, your daughter, that she may be blessed."

With a swift motion he pressed the snake's head directly on the young woman's belly. He pressed hard, and the adder bit her. With a soft moan she fainted. The boy looked at the groom and the four canopy bearers, who tried to hide their alarm.

"Be not afraid. God has turned the poison to honey."

The tableau froze for a moment. Then the bride's hand fluttered toward her face, and she came to with a gasp. The men were immensely relieved. They pressed around the boy, whose demeanor was normal now, even shy. The groom clapped him on the back.

"A son? When she comes to term, will it be a son?"

The boy nodded with a confident smile. The bride was fully revived now. The groom embraced her; somebody brought out wine to celebrate.

"Enough. Let's go," said Querulus.

He pulled Jesus away. When they were out of earshot of the wedding group, he said, "This goes on every week. They're simple people. They don't suspect that a snake can have its fangs pulled out."

"What if she has a baby and it isn't a boy?" Jesus asked.

Querulus shrugged. "They'll blame it on her. If she's unlucky, she'll be accused of adultery, and then it will go very badly for her."

The weird ritual was unsettling. As they walked out of the woods Jesus asked, "Why did you want me to see that?"

"The boy. He's you. A fake, but you all the same."

"That's crazy."

"Is it?" Querulus paused at the edge of a field and gazed up at the sun. "If Judas could use you that way, he would. He's halfway there as it is. Once he realizes that you walked out of prison and then sees you made whole again, who knows what ideas he'll come up with? Salvation isn't always about the soul. It can be a cause, and that's what he desperately needs."

Every sentence had deepened Jesus's bafflement. "I wouldn't cheat people the way that boy did. You seem to know what Judas wants from me. What do you want?"

"I'll tell you. Waiting on the fringe of every society is a savior. That's what people hunger for. A supernatural being who will make everything bad go away. Sorrow, sickness, poverty. You think your own mother doesn't pray for that?"

The mention of his mother made Jesus bite his lip. "Go on," he said curtly.

"To be a savior, you only need to know two things: human nature and the times you live in," said Querulus.

Jesus frowned. "Now you sound like Judas. I won't be used by either of you."

"Not after the first time, you mean? What if his little fraud had worked?"

Jesus looked away. However Querulus came to learn about the sham miracle in the Temple, it would have to be added to the larger enigma. Why did he care about Jesus? What made him seek out an illiterate loner from a village far to the north? Querulus read the doubts in Jesus's mind.

"You needed to see that boy in the woods," he said. "He may be a fake, but the hunger he satisfies is real. People who are starving poor find money to give to him. He passes it along to his father, who catches the snakes and runs the sorry show. They trundle in a cart from town to town. It's a going concern."

"Which has nothing to do with me," Jesus protested.

"It has something to do with all of us," Querulus shot back. He had rested barely a minute, but it was long enough for someone as restless as he was. "Come." A moment later they were striding across the fields back to town.

Jesus felt no urge to argue. Half of what Querulus said was true. Saviors were lurking in the shadows everywhere one looked. Not all were brazen enough to take on a messianic label. They passed themselves off as magi or miracle rabbis or faith healers. Jesus had been fascinated by them as a young child, until Mary and Joseph warned him that God knew the difference between pretenders and those who worked in his name. They never explained how God knew this, and Jesus forgot to ask. The miracle rabbis and wonder-workers became scarce once the Romans began to crack down harder, enforcing the laws against them. False miracles were condemned as part of the rebels' scheme to win over ignorant rural Jews.

When the edge of town came in sight, Jesus said, "Querulus sounds like a strange name. What does it mean?"

"It means a complainer."

"Is that what you are?" Whining seemed like a trait one would rather hide than advertise.

Querulus shrugged. "We take on a name to describe the state of our soul. It's like a code. My soul complains about being trapped in this world of suffering. Doesn't yours?"

"Yes." Jesus had no trouble answering quickly and simply. "If I stay, will I be given a name?"

"You already have one—'Master.' You just don't happen to like it."

Jesus didn't reply. He remembered what Querulus had said that morning about a new life, as if he naturally belonged to their group. Did he? The strange and detached state of his mind still lingered. Jesus felt no inclination to run away. In a world without peace, his soul cared very little where he went.

8

THE FOURTH MAN

The next few days were like a silent initiation. The group around Querulus wanted to inspect the newcomer. They came to the house one by one, like shy animals sneaking out of their burrows. They acted suspicious, and Jesus wondered if he had fallen into another shadow conspiracy.

A pair of nervous brothers, old sandal makers whose hands were stained with tanning fluid and gnarled like the leather they worked, had just left the house. During their visit they spent half the time staring at Jesus as if he were a monkey on a string and the other half glancing out the window.

Jesus had never met a Roman who lived intimately among the Jews. Querulus had yet to disclose what he wanted or what he was looking for. In the meantime he was aloof with those who came to the house and even showed careless disdain for them. "The spirit is willing. Too bad everything else is weak," he liked to say.

There couldn't be many patricians who, like him, had a Jewish wife. Her name was Rebekah, and Querulus was quick to point out that Herod himself wasn't a Jew, but had married into the faith. "It served his purpose, and this serves mine," he said, refusing to explain any further. If Rebekah had doubts about being the wife of a Roman, she didn't reveal them. She quietly managed the household and avoided Jesus's questioning glances. As he had suspected, she shared the house with her younger sister, Naomi, and her husband, Jacob, who seemed to have no livelihood. He spent the day shut up in a back room reading the Torah.

Inside the muted house there was no urgency. That is, except in Jesus, who went to bed every night thinking about Judas and Mary. He knew he couldn't find either one on his own. And this family never went out, preferring to live behind closed shutters and opening the door only to admit the steady stream of nervous guests on their inspection tours.

"Who are these watchers?" Jesus asked again, hoping for a more concrete answer. He had no name for the mysterious group, yet Querulus had told him that they watched and waited.

Querulus replied, "These people are like little spiders sending messages across the web. Nobody suspects them. But the real watchers are behind the scenes. You'll meet them when they're ready. They never appear unless they're ready."

"What do they do when they can't be seen?" Jesus asked.

"They serve God."

"How?"

"By praying night and day for a savior."

No more was added, but Jesus didn't like being at the center of a web, even if it served God. The nameless group wasn't a sect he was familiar with, like the Zealots or the Pharisees. Nobody conducted special rituals and prayers.

When he followed his own practices, no objection was raised. The only unusual thing was that Rebekah, called Rivka, and Naomi performed ritual bathing three times a day, and after the lavish breakfast served to him the day he arrived, their meals were sparse and plain.

Then as suddenly as the trickle of visitors had begun, it dried up. Rivka came to Jesus's room with a folded robe in her arms. She silently held it out.

"Why are you giving me this?" asked Jesus.

The robe was pure white and finely woven. Rivka turned away as soon as he took it from her. The silent message was that he had passed the test. When he showed up at the next meal wearing the gift, Querulus was obviously pleased. He poured himself a beaker of water—none of them drank wine—and without prompting began to tell his story.

He was born Quintus Tullius, the only son of a Roman citizen who had gambled on fortune the moment he set foot outside the gates of Rome, taking his family with him. His father offered no explanation for their sudden departure. But his wife, Lucilla, was weeping when she woke Quintus, then seven, in the middle of the night. The boy was confused and frightened. They hurried through the streets with cloaks over their faces. Before dawn they reached the port of Ostia, where a galley ship was waiting with its gangplank down. No other passengers got on board, and an hour later the Tullius family was huddled in the hold, heading east.

"What law did your father break?" Jesus asked.

"He did worse than break the law. He lost some important investors all their money," Querulus said.

The family fled as far as Syria, beyond the reach of angry creditors and their slaves, who had no choice but to commit murder if their masters ordered it. When Quintus got older he discovered that his father had speculated in the importation of wheat from Egypt and weevils had infected the shipment, ruining it all. His father, who had enemies, suspected that the grain was spoiled before it was loaded for export. His real enemies became imaginary ones after they settled in Antioch; gradually he became a recluse.

"Now you're one," Jesus remarked.

"No, we're not hiding in this house. We're waiting, except the wait may be over." Querulus was as enigmatic as ever, but instead of growing silent, he kept on with his story. His father found it impossible to escape the baneful influence of his imaginary enemies. His body became racked with mysterious pains; his limbs would swell without explanation; he was once found writhing on the floor with a seizure. These afflictions forced him to seek out local healers. Roman doctors were living in Syria, yet most were attached to the military, and Quintus's father suspected that they would turn him in to the proconsul and have him transported back to Rome.

Quintus was nine when shady characters began to appear on the doorstep—a stooped, one-eyed woman who nailed charms to the lintels, a family of wandering herbalists dressed in animal skins, and any number of soothsayers carting caged chickens whose entrails would be read to discover the fateful secret behind his father's maladies.

Quintus sat at his father's feet as he seized on every healer, drank every stinking potion, and took long baths in mud shipped from the banks of the Jordan or water from healing springs in Ephesus.

"He couldn't stand sunlight, which gave him piercing headaches, so I remember living in a cave that smelled of sulfur, not a house," said Querulus. Until the day came when he woke up to find dazzling morning light streaming through his bedroom window. The boy jumped out of bed and ran to the dining room, the marble-clad triclinium where the family ate their meals, month after month, without his father appearing at the table. Now he was seated in a shaft of sunlight devouring a bowl of lentils and ham.

It was the Jews who had cured him, seemingly overnight. Not with herbs, not with charms or mud, but by praying to have God remove the demon that had possessed his father's body. This miraculous recovery arrived just in time—the Tullius family fortune was all but exhausted—and his father became twice as ambitious as before. He worked his way into the army commissary and grabbed the contract for staples like onions, garlic, and olive oil.

"He knew the Jews now, and he could work with them. They weren't suspicious of him either, so it wasn't their sacred duty to cheat him the way they did the Romans," said Querulus. "He was nicknamed 'the anointed Gentile.'"

Soon a seaside villa was bought, Quintus was sent to the best tutors, and then came the arrival of a ship from Macedonia that summer. It was sailed into port by five stricken seamen whose bones showed through their flesh. The captain and the rest of the crew lay dead on deck, their bodies left to the sun and flies. The plague had come calling, a scourge that littered the streets of Antioch with thousands of corpses inside a month. It proved the downfall of the Tullius family. First his mother, then his father died before Quintus's eyes. The boy Quintus was wrapped in layers of camphor-soaked rags and hidden in the cellar. He somehow survived.

"My father didn't squander his second fortune. I had money, and it was assumed that I would sail back to Rome to live with my grandparents. But standing on the docks of Antioch, I knew I couldn't go back. That night I had a dream, and everything has followed from that, to this very day," said Querulus.

He ran his fingers lightly over Jesus's new white robe. His eyes had a faraway look, and beneath the veneer of patrician coolness, an unreadable emotion yearned for expression. Querulus was never at a loss for words, but he stumbled. "I—I have nothing more to relate. The rest is up to you."

This mystification wore out Jesus's patience. "I know why you won't tell me what you're hiding," he said. Querulus raised his eyebrows. "You're like the others, the ones who sneak into this house like thieves. You expect something from me, but you're too suspicious. You're afraid that if you say too much, I'll use your words to set a snare."

"False hope is a snare," Querulus murmured, his complexion gray with defeat.

"Then at least tell me your dream," Jesus said.

Querulus replied, "I can do better than that. I can show it to you."

He led Jesus to the back of the house, which was a jumble of small rooms added on over time, like the chambers of an ant colony, each back room getting darker and cooler than the one before it. Someone in the past had kept building on as more children were born or poor relations moved in. The last few rooms had no windows at all. Querulus had picked up an oil lamp along the way to light these black recesses.

"This was originally built as a place for women to hide themselves when they were unclean," Querulus explained curtly. "Barbaric."

He paused before a locked door and fumbled for a key. Jesus expected the last room in the warren to be the smallest, but when they stepped inside, it turned out to be large and airy, with a sizable window. Through it he spied a secret garden with green palm trees, climbing jasmine, and a bubbling fountain.

Querulus was amused by his surprise. "A pocket paradise. But that's not my dream."

He waited while their eyes adjusted to the light, then pointed to a chair against one wall. It was covered with a brocaded cloth. "Go ahead, lift it and see what's under."

Jesus pulled one edge of the cloth, which fell away. The chair beneath it was made of carved sandalwood, its fragrance adding to the heavy sweetness of jasmine in the air. On the velvet seat of the chair lay something astonishing—a gold crown.

"You stole this?" Jesus whispered. The crown was identical to the one he saw on coins stamped with the head of Herod Antipas. The circlet of gold was thick and heavy, with an inset row of jewels. However, if one looked closely, there was an empty hole where the center jewel should have been.

Querulus looked bemused. "I didn't commit treason. This is a copy. I had it hammered out in Antioch. You can touch it if you want."

Although he had never set eyes on anything remotely this splendid, Jesus instinctively kept his hand off the crown. The crown of roses that had infected him was a cautionary memory, yet something more powerful told him not to touch.

Querulus didn't seem to mind. He picked up the crown and stroked the inset gems, as if this made the wash of memories more vivid. "On the day I ran away from the steward who was appointed to take me back to Rome, I crept through the crowds back to my parents' house. An old maid was sitting on the doorstep, wringing her hands at the misfortune that had befallen her, since she now had nowhere to go. I promised to keep her with me if we could sell some of the treasures inside and find a place for me to hide.

"That night I slept in a stifling storage room in the slums of Antioch. Even though my parents had been dead less than a month, I was quivering with excitement. I felt something one isn't supposed to feel as a Roman: religious awe. I don't know where it came from. I only remember lying there feeling that my body might explode with feverish anticipation. *He* was coming for me. That's what my inner sense told me.

"But nothing happened. After midnight I fell asleep—for hours or just minutes, I don't know—until a light opened my eyes. I was confused, but ecstatic. I jumped out of bed and threw open the window. But the light of God didn't stream in. Instead, the whole neighborhood was on fire! The open window attracted the flames, and I jumped back to keep from being burned. I was frantic and ran for the door.

"In the darkness I hadn't noticed a man in the shadows, but now he blocked my escape. Before I could cry out, he said, 'Look again.' His voice was very calm, and my panic relented. I turned back to the window, and the view had magically expanded. I could see the whole city on fire and beyond that, flames licked at the horizon. 'The world's on fire,' I said in awe.

"Then a realization hit me. I whirled around to the stranger, who was dressed in a white robe and wore a gold crown. 'Do something!' I cried. I knew with total certainty that only he could save the world.

"He shook his head. 'My time hasn't come. But a few know of me already. Watch and wait. Prepare the way.'

"He emitted such a wave of love that I ran to embrace him with a heart more full than it had ever been toward my own father and mother. My arms never touched his body, but closed around empty air. At that moment I awoke in bed. Under the dream's influence, I ran to the window and threw open the shutters. Outside was the dark alley. I startled two stray cats fighting over a half-eaten rat."

Silence descended on the two of them after Querulus finished his story. After a few silent minutes, Querulus noticed something. "You're trembling."

Jesus didn't deny it. His hands were shaking; his face was drained of color.

With a peaceful quietness Querulus pushed the crown toward him. "Touch it. I can't die without my dream coming true."

Jesus knew then that the gift of the white robe was the first step, and this was the second. "What if your dream destroys me?" he asked weakly.

"It won't. It can't." Querulus was pleading now. When Jesus still recoiled, he said, "You know the world's on fire, don't you? I can't be entirely wrong about you."

Against his will, Jesus nodded.

Seeing that his young guest was bathed in sweat, Querulus relented. He replaced the crown on its cushion and threw the brocaded cloth back over the chair. He handed the oil lamp to Jesus, so that he could find his way back, and left the room. An hour later, when Jesus reappeared, nothing was said about the incident.

If the family noticed that he was still wearing the white robe and took that as a sign, no one commented on it. The very next day, Jesus disappeared.

THE ONLY THING Jesus did was step out of an ordinary house into a bustling dirty street. But for the first time in his life he was completely alone. Every face was a stranger's, every wall a secret barrier. He didn't know the name of the place or where he should go. To turn back to Nazareth was the most dangerous choice, by far.

But he couldn't stay with Querulus anymore. That much was certain. The haughty old Roman had become infected with the Jewish disease: signs and portents. Because he couldn't stand the horrors of life, he sought divine messages, a wink from God that said, "I understand. I'm coming." Standing on the threshold, Jesus didn't know whether to say "I'm sorry" or "I pity you." Half a street away, he realized what he should have said to Querulus. *"No one is coming."*

Jesus kept to the shady side of the street, wandering from one cluster of crumbling mud houses to the next. In the shadows his gleaming white robe wasn't as shocking, but still caught every passing eye.

He disbelieved Querulus's dream, but it had affected him. After the story, he had lingered in the room staring at the brocade-covered chair, which was a kind of altar, really. Querulus worshiped his fantasies there.

Noon passed. Jesus stopped by a shallow bubbling spring around which a cistern had been built. He spoke to the empty air. "If you're following me, let's all rest."

He drank a ladle of water and sat down with his back against the cistern. If the watchers were tracking him, he hoped they could see that he was hungry. One halting old man leading a donkey came up to water his animal. He nodded, maybe with a certain significance. Jesus couldn't be sure; the gesture was too brief. The man could have been one of the timid visitors to the house. Jesus almost spoke to him.

Between the sun and his hunger he dozed. Hours slipped by. The clatter of wagon wheels woke him up. The sun was low, and workers from the fields had returned to the safety of the walled town. Rough men stripped to the waist bathed in the cistern, casting suspicious glances at Jesus.

"Brother, are you needing the way back to the road?" one of them asked. It was a suggestion and a threat. The man's muscles looked like ropy knots under his sun-baked skin.

"I need a meal and a roof for the night," Jesus replied mildly. As he got to his feet, his joints ached from lying against stone.

"Nothing like that here," another man grunted.

In the glaring silence, Jesus walked away.

Hostility didn't surprise him. When he'd opened his mouth, they'd heard his accent, so it could have been worse. They could have seized him and rubbed dirt into his offending new robe or knocked him out and shouted for Roman guards.

He hung his head to avoid notice, and after a while the puffs of dust grew thicker around his sandals. The main road was approaching. When a bird's shadow passed overhead, the slanting sunlight made it look immense. Jesus gazed up and saw a starved crow settling on a low roofline. It stared arrogantly and hunched its shoulders, adjusting its metallic feathers but not flying away. For some reason Jesus was reminded of Judas. In the last few days, Jesus hadn't given much thought to either Judas or Mary. Now, for a reason he could not name, he realized that he had to reject them as companions and continue to move on by himself. Perhaps it was the same disease—signs and portents—that made them expect too much, more than he could ever give. He had to find a place that wasn't infected, and the only way to find one was alone.

Oblivion might have swallowed up the rest of the story, except for the smallest turn of fate. With the village behind him, a blast of heat made Jesus raise his head. It was as if high noon had returned at dusk. He saw a small, agitated crowd up ahead. Men shouting and waving their arms ran past him. An outlying house in the village stood between Jesus and the setting sun. It shimmered and swam in the air, and suddenly he realized why: the house was on fire. The flames were made invisible by the sun's greater light.

More men ran past, sloshing buckets of water. Women wailed. There was no well nearby. The house had been built too far from town. Someone screamed out a name, then another. They were trying to locate the family who belonged to the house; a terrible suspicion grew that they were still inside, silenced by heat and smoke.

The running men stumbled over Jesus and cursed him when they did. He had sunk to his knees in the middle of the road, transfixed by the fire. Images flashed in his mind of the Nazarene house that the Romans had set to the torch, and Isaac's relatives who had perished inside. Querulus's dream was springing to life.

But these powerful thoughts were not what mesmerized him. Jesus heard the trapped family calling him.

As clearly as if he could see through the mud walls now streaked with soot, he spied a mother and two young daughters. They were huddled in a corner, too far away from a window to run for it, sealed off by fire that licked its way up the walls to the tinderbox wooden ceiling. Jesus heard them call again, but not for the father—he must be the man who had tried to run into the inferno but was held back by three stronger friends. The father struggled to break free, a tortured silhouette against the sun and fire.

Jesus! Jesus!

The trapped ones were screaming his name. For a moment he knelt and listened. A wave of fear should have coursed through him. It didn't. Jesus knew that the place he had to find, the one place that wasn't infected, the center of purity, lay before him.

It was the fire.

Rising to his feet, he headed straight for it. "Hey, stop him! Are you crazy!"

The shouts reached his ears from far away. The fire had become too intense for anyone to stand near it anymore. Nobody thought to seize the stranger the way they had seized the desperate father for his own good. Jesus smiled. Not at the nearness of death or because the heat made his facial muscles constrict, but because a picture had come to mind.

He saw three men in a furnace singing God's praises. He couldn't name what book they were in or much of their story. A wicked king had thrown them, three inseparable young friends, into a fiery furnace. But instead of burning to a crisp, they stood there and laughed and sang. As a boy Jesus had gone around for several days muttering their names under his breath like a holy chant: *Shadrach, Meshach, Abednego.* It wasn't an easy chant when you were five years old, and he was proud of himself for getting it right.

He muttered it now, wondering if the sound would guide his soul to Nazareth one last time before it flew to Paradise.

Shadrach, Meshach, Abednego.

All the women screamed when the stranger in the luminous white robe strode into the raging fire. He got past the front door just as the lintel beam crashed to earth, weakened by the falling walls. More of the roof caved in, and through the hole that was made flames shot higher into the sky, like demons released from their cage.

As for what happened next, the young man who walked out with the mother and children safe under his cloak, like a dove sheltering new fledgling chicks under its wings, wasn't the only one who knew the story of the fiery furnace. People spoke about it throughout the village that night, in between the celebrations for the rescued family, who were dazed but unharmed, thanks to God.

Around the rabbi's table the story was told most accurately, of course. In the reign of Nebuchadnezzar, the noblest sons of Israel were captured and brought back to Babylon. Daniel and three friends were among them; their fate was to be treated as honored captives. They would be trained in foreign ways—perhaps even inducted into the mysteries of the magi—and learn to devote themselves to a foreign god.

But when Nebuchadnezzar erected an idol and decreed that everyone in the city should bow down to it whenever they heard the sound of flute, zither, and lyre, the three friends refused. The king grew furious and ordered that a furnace be built especially to burn them alive. On the appointed day the furnace was fired seven times hotter than normal, so hot that the soldiers who threw the condemned into it were burned to death themselves.

After a time Nebuchadnezzar ordered the furnace door to be opened, but when he looked inside, Shadrach, Meshach, and Abednego were alive and walking around, surrounded by flame. The king fell back in awe and released them on the spot. Everyone in the village knew that part, but the rabbi remembered a forgotten detail.

"There was a fourth man inside that furnace when it was opened, but only three had been put in. You understand?" The rabbi took another long drink of wine and gestured for his wife to pass around the platter of roasted haunch of goat one more time. It had been a miraculous day and fitting to God that they treat it as such. "Scripture tells us he was no ordinary man, but looked like *a son of the gods*."

Later, and a little drunk, the rabbi called for his scrolls to be unwrapped, and he pointed to the passage in the book of Daniel. His eyes watered up.

"I don't have to tell you why I remember this detail. Do you have any doubt who came out of that fire today? Three, and a fourth." He lapsed into a significant silence so that his words could hang in the air. Three, and a fourth.

Which was how the miracle was remembered after he died and the story passed on to his sons and their sons after them.

9

SECOND BIRTH

Walking into the fire had been easy. His body remained calm, trembling only slightly when the heat became intense. Gazing at the flames, he heard a voice say, "*My son*."

This voice seemed to come from the fire itself, in a beckoning whisper like the hiss of dry leaves burning. He followed the whisper, and with each step the heat eased, even as the wind whipped his hair wildly about.

My son.

The two words made him safe. When he stepped into the heart of the inferno, nothing could harm him.

The woman and her two children cowering in the corner had pulled their black woolen scarves over their faces to keep from suffocating. Only their eyes were visible, wide and terrified. Jesus had never seen anyone so terrified by the nearness of death. He then realized that they were afraid of him, not the fire. The smaller girl cringed when he gathered her in his arms.

She clung to her mother. "Don't let him kill me," she begged.

The mother, overcome with smoke and fear, allowed Jesus to wrap his arms around the three of them. He took them through the flames, and a moment later they emerged. The small crowd fell back; water buckets dropped to the ground. The husband cried out his wife's name. She rushed into his arms, dragging her children behind her. Nobody made a move toward Jesus, though. They were frozen with awe. The only sound was the sobbing of the husband and his bewildered family. Strangely, Jesus still wanted to walk down the road, the same thing he'd wanted before he set eyes on the burning house.

He had to move through the crowd to get back to the road. He kept his eyes forward, not looking to either side. Then the strange hypnotic spell suddenly broke. People cried out. Hands reached for Jesus, and there was no way to stop them. He wrapped his arms around himself to keep his white cloak from being snatched off his back. The hands wanted to seize the miracle, to tear away a piece that could be saved and hoarded.

One pair, Jesus noticed, was more gnarled than the others. It belonged to a bent, wizened old woman. "Do you have a barn?" Jesus asked. He had no idea why he picked her. She nodded.

"Take me there," he said. He gently touched the old woman's hands, and amazement crossed her face. She shouted in the local dialect, waving away the others. Whatever the cry meant, they backed off, and she led Jesus away from the road. The old woman mumbled in disbelief and couldn't stop looking at her hands. They crossed a small field by way of a narrow path, and behind a screen of cypress trees there was a small barn.

"You don't want to come into the house?" The old woman fixed on him quizzically and pointed toward a sun-baked mud dwelling beyond the barn.

He shook his head and went into the barn, fading into its cool shadows. She knew not to follow him. An angel of mercy can suddenly turn into the angel of death if God wills it.

Inside, the sheep manure was pungent. His entry caused some lambs to bleat. After a second his eyes adjusted, and Jesus saw two ewes penned up with their newborns. Their prudent owner wanted to shelter them for a few days before exposing the lambs to the wild. Jesus noticed a ladder leading up to a loft where what remained of last year's hay was stored. He climbed up and lay down.

I am the son.

The words came clearly, without effort, and he believed them, feeling the last gold rays of daylight fall on his face. The sun was setting through cracks in the sagging timber roof. The air in the barn was musty and cold. Jesus wondered why he wasn't struck with amazement. He had done nothing to become the son, any more than a baby causes itself to be born. But like a baby, he had emerged from some kind of invisible darkness, and the world was reborn with him.

If God had any further explanation, he kept it to himself. The ewes moved toward a small manger filled with fresh hay and began to chew. The lambs jumped around, too frisky to sleep. Jesus must have slept, however, because the next thing he knew, there was a thump against the mud wall down below. It was too dull to wake him up, but another thump followed, then a third. He rolled over on his side and peered through a crack in the wall. In the gray-blue dimness before dawn some villagers had found him; they were throwing rocks at the barn. Several more hit with the same dull thud. The sheep bleated nervously. Jesus came wide awake.

As he climbed down the ladder, he didn't wonder what mood would greet him. The people would be joyous and awe-struck. The miracle of the day before told them who he was.

Why, then, did the villagers scowl when he came to the barn door? Several of the men had lifted new rocks, and instead of dropping them, they held them at the ready.

One shouted, "Who are you?"

Jesus recognized him as the angry workman bathing at the cistern. One of the poised rocks got thrown, and it barely missed Jesus's chest. The man had taken a wild shot; he couldn't see well in the predawn dimness.

"Who are you?" the voice repeated, harsher and louder.

Jesus turned away. His first impulse had been right; he should be walking the road, not lingering here. The road was his vanishing point, his salvation. Without looking behind, he felt the villagers follow him. They kept quiet, scowling. It was clear that it would be good enough if the intruder, God-sent or Devil-sent, just disappeared. His feet found the narrow path across the field. Jesus walked it without rushing, and the small band tailed him single file. They made a strange sight, like a hen and chicks, all in a row.

The main road appeared. Jesus heard no one behind him. The villagers stopped, waiting until he was out of sight. Each step brought a new sensation, not relief, but a swelling rage in his chest.

Jesus whirled around. The knot of people now stood just over ten paces away.

"Who am I?" he said with cold fury. "I am the light!"

God, who was in a merciful mood the day before, had a whim to be mischievous now. Like the manager of cheap theatrics, God drew aside a thin veil of clouds. If cymbals had been at hand, they would have added a splendid effect. As it was, the sun fell upon Jesus's white cloak the very instant he uttered the word "light." What could his onlookers do? Their suspicion and petty anger were flimsy nothings, swept away by a flood of awe.

They committed blasphemy by uttering Yahweh's name, falling to their knees in the dust. Their mouths gaped open, and Jesus couldn't help but see the image of a hen and chicks again.

You shall feed them.

Like the words from the fire, these came from the sunlight that made Jesus's robe almost too dazzling to look at. He listened and nodded. It was so easy. The light had come to him, and he would give the light to them. He crossed the small distance between himself and the villagers. One man was so dazed that his fist still clutched a rock. Jesus took it away and threw it in the air. Every eye followed its arc until it plunked to earth far down the road.

"I am the light." This time Jesus said it gently, without a trace of anger. The man who had been clutching the rock started to cry. Jesus touched the man's shoulder. Tears drew dirty streaks down his cheeks, and his chest heaved.

As easy as it was to walk into the fire, to be the son and give the light, Jesus was now at a loss to understand the magnitude and limits of his gift. He no longer felt the call of the road. He needed to find out what all this meant, and to do that, he had to return to town.

• • •

THE FIRST PUBLIC place he came to was the town cistern. Word had clearly spread. The women who were filling their water pitchers fled as soon as Jesus appeared. The earliest workers had already come and gone, but that still left a dozen men. Without looking at them Jesus took off his cloak, folded it neatly, and put it on the shelf of the cistern wall (sending up a small prayer that nobody would steal it). Stripped to the waist, he waded into the water and washed himself. Two day's grime and soot from the fire caked his skin.

"What do you see?" he asked, not fixing his eyes on anyone in particular. "How am I different from you?" The crowd didn't answer. One of the street urchins kicking a ball on the fringes shouted, "You don't belong here!"

"Is that why you sent these men to stone me?" Jesus nodded toward the knot of attackers who had followed him from the edge of town. "Not for any sin or blasphemy, but because you imagine I am different?" The cool water running down his bare arms made him shiver. "Moses was a stranger in a strange land. If you are his children, so am I. Would you now make me a stranger?"

Still no one spoke, but he sensed that his listeners were relenting, just slightly, like a leather bow string that must relax or snap when it has been taut too long.

"How did you walk through fire?" someone asked.

"No man can walk through fire, but the spirit can. I have no other explanation," said Jesus.

"Rubbish. You're a magician, and half of them are possessed by demons. Why should we trust you?" Onlookers were stirring now, more willing to voice their suspicions.

Jesus looked at the one who spoke up, a swarthy, squat muscular man in a leather apron. A blacksmith. Jesus saw that he was angry and had been all his life. What could he say that would penetrate that armor? Every man there lived behind a wall as thick as the town's ancient rampart. Jesus paused, then he took a small clay jug—half a dozen lay around for public use.

"See?" he said. He scooped water into the jug and held it high. "This water is like the holy spirit." He slowly tilted the jug and let its contents stream over his head. "If I let the spirit rain over me, it makes me pure and clean. But half an hour from now it will be dried up and blown away. Sweat and dirt will soil me again."

He took the jug and filled it once more, holding it close to his chest. "But if I take the same water and cover it and put it in a cool place, it will last for days. You all know this." Jesus waited to see what effect his words would have.

"Explain your meaning," someone called out impatiently.

"Your heart is like this jug—fill it with the holy spirit and keep it inside yourself. Then it won't dry up and blow away. One day you will be amazed, for God knows where your secret places are. When you least expect it, the jug will overflow, and then you will walk through fire or do anything you want. Nothing is impossible when the spirit is full within."

There were some astonished whispers mixed with grumbling. Jesus paid no attention. He climbed out and wrapped his cloak around his half-naked body. "You have a right to know who I am. I am Jesus, from Nazareth. One or two of you have the same name. If not you, your brother or cousin. But a name means nothing. I will answer to it if you call me, but my soul won't. It abides with God and answers only when he calls."

A low hum of approval went through the bystanders, all but canceling out the grumbles. Jesus smiled to himself. It had become easy to say the truth since his new birth. He couldn't even find the part of himself that used to be afraid of the truth. One of the older men, grayer than the others and probably poorer to judge by the mends in his brown robe, came forward. "Visit my house. Let me feed you," he said.

"Why?" Jesus asked.

"Because you're hungry," the man said. "You'd rather starve?"

Jesus smiled and patted the man's shoulder, which was more bone than flesh. "I'll go with you. You've come to me in peace. Let us feast."

"Oh no, don't expect a feast," the old man mumbled, his lip quivering.

"I must expect one, and so must you. How else would our Father want us to live, if he truly loves us?"

The bystanders were jostling around them, and they all heard what Jesus said. He put his arm around the old man's shoulders and walked down the nearest alley. No one followed except the street urchins, and they had no idea what happened once the two disappeared behind the door of the old man's hovel. Rumors are the fuel of wonder, however, and soon the whole town was quite certain. The old man had opened his cupboard, which that morning held only a cracked jug of water and half a loaf of stale bread wrapped in a dirty rag. But now, a feast tumbled out. All the townspeople saw it in their mind's eye. They vicariously ate the delicious sweetmeats that poured out and emptied the wine cask that the stranger had filled.

One thing is for certain, instead of napping, everyone was kept awake by excitement during the long afternoon except for the old man himself. He slept all day and through the night. When the morning sun struck his thin eyelids, he found his visitor was gone.

BEFORE DAWN JESUS went into the hills to wait. God had lifted him up and carried him very far, but he knew God's ways. Whenever he exalted a son of Adam, what came next was always the same. Catastrophe, a fall, a shattering crash. Moses had been lifted highest of all (not counting Lucifer), to what end? His people were saved. They arrived at the land of milk and honey. Out of all the wandering, starved, despised, and exhausted multitudes, Moses alone was denied the final reward.

Jesus stood on a rise overlooking the town. Down below wisps of smoke rose from house fires; a few lanterns twinkled in the sleepy windows. Moses had died on a mountaintop after one last look at the promised land. Knowing that he was condemned, he could still bless the children of Israel—his children, who would outlive him in tears and sorrow. Then old Moses climbed to the summit of Pisgah to perish alone.

"Do what you will, Father," Jesus called aloud. "But if you love me, bury me yourself when it's done." The wind whipped harder and whistled in his ear.

"Will I die so full of sin that you will renounce me completely?"

Jesus didn't believe that the empty air heard him. But scripture said that God buried Moses with his own hands in an unmarked grave. Jesus gazed at the desert scrub, which was browner and more sparse than the fragrant pinewoods he knew at home.

A tiny quiver caught his eye. A nearby rock had trembled. No, it was a hare. The whole time Jesus had been arguing with God, the poor creature—a sad, scrawny gray excuse of a hare—had frozen stock-still, trying not to breathe. Finally it couldn't help itself and had released one shiver of fear.

"Go in peace," Jesus murmured.

The hare darted off in a quick burst, as if shot by a spring. It didn't care about going in peace, just getting away without a broken neck.

Jesus watched the puffs of dust the hare's thumping feet kicked up. A day from the past came to mind when he had sat on a rock sunning himself with Isaac. He must have been all of ten.

"You're quiet. What are you watching?" the blind man asked.

"A rabbit. It can't decide whether to run away or not."

The rabbit, a small fat female, was watching them anxiously, tempted to come closer by a tuft of sweet April grass.

"What's hunting it, a fox or a weasel?" Isaac asked.

Until then, the boy Jesus hadn't noticed a predator around. Isaac's keen hearing picked up something, the snap of the smallest twig, maybe. Jesus squinted into the distant brightness.

"A fox," he said. He picked up a rock and hurled it at the fat rabbit, which darted away in panic. The fox, which hadn't crawled close enough for a chase, emitted a disgusted yip. It waved its brushy tail in their faces and trotted off.

"Always on the side of the innocent," Isaac remarked. There was a tone in his voice. Jesus was surprised.

"She was defenseless," he said.

"So?" Isaac lifted his eyebrows. "You want to protect the innocent. Let me tell you, God isn't just in the rabbits. He's also in the foxes. So your little act of kindness deprived God of a meal."

Jesus laughed, conceding the point. But he was stung nevertheless. Isaac could tell.

"I'm not teasing you, boy. I worry about these things every day. The innocent, the guilty. The hunter, the hunted. If God is just, why do the meek shed their blood while the vicious grow fat?"

Isaac said nothing more. The day was hot for spring. He held his hand up to shade his shriveled eyelids ringed with puckered red folds of skin.

"We should be getting back," Jesus said. He reached for the blind man's arm, but Isaac resisted, keeping his sightless eyes fixed on the sun.

"God's light sometimes burns me," he said. "That's no reason to run away from it."

Now Jesus wished he could go back to that moment, because he knew just what to say. "Don't worry anymore. The innocent and the guilty, the hunter and the hunted. There is no need to judge them. God wants to save them all."

Jesus headed back to town. The first person he saw was a youth stabbing at a parched field with a broken spade. When he set eyes on Jesus, the youth stiffened.

"What can I do for you, rabbi?" he said. He kept his head down and his voice low. Word had spread everywhere.

"I need a guide," said Jesus. "But you must take me through the most deserted streets you can find. Are there places set aside for the sick and dying?"

The youth nodded.

"That way, then," said Jesus. "And don't be afraid, but I have to go where the holy women are."

The youth looked confused; he didn't know that lingo.

"The women who walk with men when God isn't looking," said Jesus. He smiled, but the youth turned red and couldn't stammer out a reply. Without a word he pointed the way to a narrow crack of an opening in the village wall. Soon they were creeping down lanes too narrow even to be alleys. All the houses were shuttered, but Jesus heard faint moans and smelled a stench of vomit and dying flesh. With a wordless blessing he promised to return. For now, he let the youth lead him, spying around corners to make sure no one was outdoors before waving Jesus on.

The brothel area was close by. It smelled worse than the streets of the dying, because heavy sweet perfume mingled with residues of the rotting stench. The youth waited for Jesus to catch up.

"I can't go any farther," he said. Where the boy had taken him was forbidden, but it would be worth it when he ran back and told everyone his tale. He started to back away, but Jesus held him by the nape of his neck through his coarse robe. "I am not here to sin," he said.

"Of course, rabbi." The youth discreetly kept his eyes toward the ground, but he couldn't hide a faint smile.

"Look at me," Jesus said. "If the town drives me away because of you, there will be no more miracles. You understand?"

A stubborn stare came into the boy's eyes. "Where's my miracle?" he said, wheedling.

Had it come to that already, in less than a day? Jesus would have wrapped the collar tighter around the youth's neck, but then he realized. They weren't his miracles to give or take away. He closed his eyes and waited.

Through him words came out.

"Your grandmother will not die this season. She will rise from her bed in a week."

Perhaps the youth's eyes widened; a cry of gratitude may have swelled his throat. But Jesus had already turned aside and was marching toward the first house on the street, its painted door decorated with a blue snake coiled around an erect phallus. A Roman sign. The main customers would be soldiers, and they wouldn't be able to read Hebrew.

"Master!"

The youth was calling after him, but Jesus didn't look back. Even if God had spoken through him, it made him sick to barter with miracles. He stopped at the door and knocked. No one opened it, but a woman's voice called from inside.

"Too early. The girls are asleep. Come back at noon."

Jesus knocked again, harder, and after a pause the door opened a crack. A short woman with henna in her hair and an uncovered face appeared. When she saw that Jesus was a Jew, she hurriedly drew her sleeve across all but her eyes. "Didn't you hear me?"

"I'm here for Mary. Bring her to the door."

The woman, who must have been the procuress, became suspicious. "She's not here, and she ain't seeing nobody. Not till noon."

"Bring her."

Jesus had been guided to the town, but didn't need a divine message to seek Mary out in the brothel quarter. It only made sense that she needed some way to survive.

But now he smelled, through the sweet perfume mixed with the rotting stench, something else. A mixture of saffron, cumin, and coriander that was familiar, because Mary had carried a packet of those spices with her when she fled Jerusalem. A dozen times on the road she had sprinkled them on the fish heads and lamb entrails that her copper coins had bought for dinner.

"I know she's here. I can smell something."

"We're here to smell it too," a man said angrily. "Up close. So get out of the way, Jew." The voice came from behind him, and it was Roman. Jesus turned around and faced two infantry soldiers. They were disheveled and drunk. The one who spoke leered at him.

The procuress gave them an oily smile. Regular customers. She opened the door and bowed. Jesus didn't move aside, however.

The other soldier became truculent. "Didn't we tell you to shove off?" His hand went to the handle of the sword hanging by his side, but his companion, who was in a better mood, clapped Jesus on the shoulder.

"He don't mean it. Go in. We're all brothers beyond this blue door, ain't we?"

The procuress, who was anxious not to have a fight on her hands, yanked Jesus inside. Caught off guard, he stumbled over the threshold, pushed from behind by the impatient legionaries. One could hear the low talk of girls in the next room, punctuated by giggles. Even in the dim light the procuress could see that the soldiers' faces were growing red and urgent. She called out, "Get ready. Uncover yourselves, darlings. Early gentlemen."

She drew aside a curtain, revealing a low divan covered with sheepskin rugs. Lounging on it were two girls, caught by surprise without their heavy makeup. They let out timid shrieks, and the soldiers burst out laughing. One ran to the couch and began pulling up one girl's flimsy shift to expose her legs.

It felt like a dream to Jesus, a flickering appearance. He wasn't embarrassed, even as the scene became lurid and the girls reached out to grab for him. Jesus turned slowly, with the dreamlike sensation that he was a phantom, and then he saw who it was. Mary had entered the room. She was dressed in a coarse robe with an apron tied around her waist, a wooden spoon in her hands.

You. Mary's mouth formed the syllable without speaking.

Being dressed like a cook didn't protect her, however. One of the drunken soldiers caught sight of her. "That one!" he cried, pushing aside the naked girl who was clinging to him. He lurched forward from the divan stripped down to his linen undergarment, not hiding his aroused state. Mary looked away. She didn't want to meet the soldier's avid, greedy eyes, and she couldn't look into Jesus's.

Jesus had said nothing, had barely moved, but his presence irritated the Roman. "Best leave us alone, Jew. Unless she's your sister, you don't belong here." With a rough paw he shoved Jesus toward the door.

The sensation of moving in a dream still held as Jesus watched his hand ball into a fist and swing through the air. It struck the soldier's jaw silently, but at that instant Jesus heard a loud crack as the bone broke. Blood spurted from the soldier's mouth and his eyes turned to saucers as he went down.

The next sound was Mary's voice. "Quick!"

The other Roman roared like a bull and staggered to his feet. Jesus caught a glimpse of gleaming steel as a sword was drawn from its scabbard. But Mary had already pulled him out into the street, running barefoot over rocks and refuse, and even though the roaring continued behind them, a naked legionary who had just tripped over his fallen comrade wasn't likely to give pursuit.

10

CAPTIVE

Mary was still running when Jesus held her back. "We can walk away," he said. "I am watched over."

"You weren't before. You wound up in jail," she said, looking back nervously at the brothel. "I couldn't stay in that place. A farmer brought me here in his cart." She pulled her shawl over her face. So far, nobody had rushed out after them.

"Listen and hear me. I am watched over," said Jesus.

His calmness shocked her. He had lashed out in anger a moment ago, but the storm passed as quickly as it arose. Wherever Jesus had been hiding, he had found new clothes and lost the air of a fugitive. Mary tried to will her heart to stop racing with panic. She glanced down at his right hand. The knuckles were oozing red from breaking the Roman's jaw.

"You're bleeding," she said.

"A little."

Jesus ignored the wound. He had his mind on other things, in particular the scrabbling crowds that would soon swarm around him. As soon as they reached the main part of town, he and Mary wouldn't be able to talk together. He took her hands.

"You don't have anything to explain. I know you didn't go back to what you did before."

Mary met his gaze steadily; her lips didn't tremble. "I thought I'd never see you again. I waited in a hiding place. I was too afraid to search for you. Judas is a coward, so I knew he'd run away. I gave a coin to a boy on the street, and he ran to spy around the jail. He told me that the quarantine was lifted and everyone let go."

"Judas isn't a coward," Jesus said. "He's canny. I imagine he ran some place underground."

Mary looked bitter. "He abandoned us both. What else matters? I'm relieved you didn't run away with him."

There was an awkward pause, and then Mary said, "You came for me. What are you going to do with me now?"

Jesus was startled. "Help you. What else?"

"You really don't know?"

When Jesus didn't reply, Mary said, "No man will have me anymore. I'm like an apple core once the fruit is eaten. You must know that much, at least."

Jesus looked away. "I don't think about that."

"Well, you should. You've gone through too much to be a boy anymore." Mary sounded almost angry. "When you and Judas kept me with you, you tainted yourself with a fallen woman. Don't deny it."

Jesus hung his head. "You are outside the law. We both know that."

"And where are you, inside the law?" She didn't wait for a reply. "Do you think I'm Eve? I didn't disobey. I was forced outside God's blessing, and now any man can do with me as he wants. That's why I asked what you're going to do with me."

Jesus had to face the truth. He had no idea why he kept trying to find Mary. He would never marry her, and therefore it was forbidden in the commandments to keep company with her. Was it his conscience that made him refuse to let her go? No, because he had walked past dozens of fallen women on the road—beggars, whores, the sick and lame—without taking them up.

He said, "I told you I wanted to help you, but that's not the whole truth. I *must* help you. I don't know how, but I can't let you go until I find out."

By now a band of street urchins had spotted him; they ran away emitting shrill whistles to alert the town.

Soberly he said, "I want you to know the truth. You almost didn't see me again. I was walking away when it happened."

Mary didn't ask what "it" meant, so she must have heard about the miracle at the burning house. Could she tell that he had changed overnight? It was impossible that she didn't see it.

For the first time she seemed to suppress a feeling of shame. Her eyes dropped, and she said, "You should walk away now."

"No."

"They'll drive you out if you're seen with me."

Jesus lifted her head. "Too late. God already sees you with me."

Mary said nothing, allowing Jesus to pull her down the street by the hand, ignoring the open stares of strangers who were starting to emerge from the shadowy alleys and side streets.

"You belong out here, in the light," said Jesus. "I was weak before. I had my doubts, but not anymore. Stay with me."

His tone of voice baffled her. "You're the first man to speak to me this way since—"

"Since your fiancé was betrayed to the Romans," said Jesus. "God saw you weep. He saw everything."

"Then why did he let me—" Finishing the sentence was too painful. Her tears began to flow.

Jesus said, "I don't know what God intended. Here, wipe your cheeks. They'll think you have something to be ashamed of."

Erasing the steaks of her tears with her sleeve, Mary shook her head. If she had wanted to speak, she would have been quickly drowned out. A throng was closing in from all sides, gathering faster than she could have imagined. Voices clamored, "Master, master! Over here!"

Jesus barely had time to lean close and whisper, "God made something innocent in you that nothing can touch. Love that part, as I love it."

Hands were pulling Jesus away now, tugging at his robe and arms. A wailing peasant woman threw herself between him and Mary, screaming incoherently. Once the wedge was made, they were flung apart by the surging mob. Jesus was whirled around, and although he tried to keep his eyes on Mary, she was jostled to the edge of the crowd as it thickened and swelled.

In her fear she saw the mob as a ravening beast, ready to rip Jesus apart before her eyes. The image made her shudder. But he didn't allow the beast to spring. Mary couldn't see how he did it, but with a glance Jesus made the seizing hands let go. He said something out of earshot, very softly, and a ripple went through the crowd, settling the air like a cool breeze after a thunderstorm.

When it was quiet enough to be heard, Jesus said, "Where are you taking me? Speak up." No one answered. There was no single purpose behind the mob except to get close to him.

Jesus met the eyes of the packed circle who pressed closest to him. "Even in synagogue when everyone wants to be near God, there's room to kneel."

People pushed back, and a little more space was made around him. Mary was amazed that she could hear Jesus so clearly; it was uncannily as if he still whispered in her ear. Was this happening to everyone?

Jesus spoke and the words flowed as if he had given this speech a thousand times. "I wandered the hills near my village when I was a boy. I had no idea where to go. No one expected anything of me. For all I knew, I was forgotten by God. Who hasn't been bothered this way?" He had adopted a new tone, as if reminiscing with a friend. His gaze scanned the crowd, which calmed down even more, before he continued. "One day I was exhausted with worry, and my feet were cut and bruised by rocks. I sank to the ground under a tree.

"I only intended to be there a moment, when I spied a sparrow. It flitted to one spot in the dirt and pecked at a grass seed. A second later it flitted to another spot, then another. In my eyes there was no pattern to its action, just a witless sparrow zigging and zagging, getting nowhere.

"Suddenly my eyes were opened. How many generations of sparrows have lived this way? Many more than the generations of men. They had no plan where they were going. But God's hand has guided them these thousands of years. If he can find seed enough for sparrows, what more does he want to do for you?"

The crowd murmured. No one had ever spoken to them this way. Jesus raised his voice. "I ask again, where are you taking me? If you don't know, then release me. I am only God's sparrow. He must want me to zig and zag some more before he tells me what to do."

With some mumbling but no resistance the crowd parted; a path was cleared for Jesus to escape. As soon as he came to the end of the path, it closed behind him, and the crowd followed in his wake. Mary was left at the rear among the stragglers. From around the corner a Roman patrol suddenly appeared, coming in their direction. She was almost certain she didn't recognize either of the soldiers from the brothel, but she walked faster and melted into the crowd.

Mary thought she heard one of the soldiers say, "Should we break them up, sergeant?"

There was a gruff reply, but nothing more. She stole a glance backward. The patrol hung back, trailing the crowd with weapons sheathed. They looked indecisive—it would be futile to disperse a mob that outnumbered them by more than ten to one.

Up ahead Jesus walked casually, as if he were alone and without direction. The crowd followed, until they came to the open market entrance and a familiar figure. As soon as they laid eyes on him, the crowd rumbled angrily. It was a squat Roman in a dirty toga sitting on a stool. He was positioned to watch anyone who came or went. Between his legs was a leather bag, in front of him a small table set up as a writing desk.

"Don't go near him, master," a voice called out.

Jesus turned in its direction. "Why not?"

"You'll just be robbed. He's a thief!"

Jesus regarded the squat Roman, who resembled the tax collectors he knew from Nazareth. Perched by the shore where the fishing boats came in or situated at the mouth of the market, their presence was as predictable as vultures.

"Do you despise this man?" he asked, not waiting for the chorus of boos that answered him. "I know as well as you what the Romans have done to us. It's time to pay them back. Who has a coin?"

The crowd was baffled. A coin? They expected Jesus to command them to rush the tax collector and attack him. Apparently so did the squat Roman, who nervously pulled the drawstrings of his leather money purse and shoved his pens into his sleeve. Mary glanced back; the armed patrol had drawn nearer. Their weapons were drawn now.

Jesus paid no attention to the rumbling, but kept his hand out until someone placed a copper coin in it.

"Stay here."

He had enough control over the crowd that they hung back as he approached the tax collector, who had grown more nervous. He brusquely tried to wave Jesus away. "Are you bringing goods to sell? If not, you don't have to pay."

Jesus held out the coin and spoke in a low voice. "Apparently God wants us both to play our parts."

"What your god wants means nothing to me," the man hissed.

"Does staying alive mean something to you?" With a flourish Jesus dropped the coin on the tax collector's desk. The ping of the coin as it landed caused the crowd to break out in fresh boos and something more ominous, a low, angry bellow against Jesus.

"Fraud! Hypocrite!"

He turned. "Who is a hypocrite? He who obeys the law?"

"Not Caesar's law," someone called. "Only God makes laws for us."

"I see. Then God must curse you, because whoever disobeys Caesar's law will certainly be imprisoned or die. Let me ask, am I still a hypocrite or are you?" he shouted.

There was a sharp whistle from the back of the crowd. The Roman soldiers were splitting up and taking positions, calling out signals while sending for backup. From where she stood Mary could see the soldiers approach. What had made Jesus suddenly want to commit suicide?

The front ranks of the mob threatened to boil over and rush at him, but his glare kept them back.

"What did you think your messiah would do?" he shouted. "Wipe out the Romans with a magic finger?" Jesus had never uttered the word *messiah* before, but he knew the whispered rumors born of desperation. Only the crudest magicians, the kind who pulled red and green scarves out of the ears of children and simpletons, weren't called Savior of the Jews.

"The messiah wouldn't lick their asses," a man shouted back. This time it wasn't a voice lost in the crowd, but a tradesman wearing a tool apron who stepped forward.

"I will tell you the truth," Jesus said steadily, meeting the man's hostile stare. "You have no idea what the messiah would do. Neither do I." He lifted his head toward the crowd. "But here's another truth you have thrown into the dust. A great abyss stands between the kingdom of Caesar and the Kingdom of God. Have you not been told this over and over? Romans are ignorant of God's laws, so they have no choice but to lay down their own.

"Is God offended? How can he be? Worldly affairs do not touch him. The richest Roman will die unworthy to touch the hem of the least of you in Heaven. Then be as God is. Before you speak of the law, know what kingdom you belong to. Otherwise, you are no better than hypocrites."

By this time a dozen garrisoned soldiers had materialized to back up the patrol; they were positioned behind the crowd with shield and sword at the ready. Jesus had insulted the emperor and defied his authority, which was reason enough to charge forward and take him. But he had also done something else—he had quelled a mob with no more than words. The sergeant in charge hesitated; the others waited for his orders. Their main purpose was to rescue the tax collector, but Jesus now touched his shoulder and nodded. The crowd watched tensely as the squat Roman packed up his desk and scurried away through the half-deserted marketplace. In a moment he had disappeared, and the spark went out.

"Stand down!" the sergeant ordered, loud enough so that the Jews knew his men were there.

Mary held her breath. A second spark could still ignite. Riots had broken out over less. Except for a few malcontents, no one responded to the implicit threat, however. The men in front of Mary were tall, but for a moment she caught sight of Jesus between their bodies. He wore a strange expression on his face. His mouth smiled, but his eyes were sad and inward. A visible wave of exhaustion passed over Jesus as the mob dispersed, his shoulders suddenly sagging. It had cost him more to bring peace than to break a Roman's jaw.

The power of Jesus's speech had made Mary shudder. Was it dread or hope? If the latter, this was hope that might die before it drew its first breath.

• • •

THE ROMANS SUDDENLY had more trouble on their hands than another pretend messiah or whatever deluded madman the Jews were following that week. A petty official was killed as he was walking home from the public baths, stabbed from the shadows by the same kind of *kanai*, or "knife men," who caused trouble in the north. Such an occurrence was rare in the south, so when a second killing occurred—this time of a senator's profligate son who had been exiled to Judea to save him from a murder trial in Rome—the noose was tightened. For a week the open markets were closed, along with the baths. More rashly, the provincial governor ordered a guard posted to keep the Jews from attending the local synagogue. A mob rose up in fury outside the gates. The guards were stoned and barely escaped with their lives.

Any Jewish property owner retreated behind locked doors. Only the poorest sought out Jesus for help. He was no longer in town; they had to find him in the hills, where he went to pray and sleep at night. Jesus took Mary with him, which under normal circumstances would have scandalized the new followers, but the crisis at hand kept them from complaining.

For several days in a row contingents of poor besieged him. To all of them Jesus said, "What would you have me do?"

Answers shot back. "Lead an army."

"Send an earthquake."

"Call down the angel of death as Moses did. We can mark our doors with blood to show the angel we are Jews so we'll be spared. Wasn't that the lesson of Passover?"

"Moses called down nothing," said Jesus. "It was God's will. The lesson of Passover is that he decides."

When his beseechers went away grumbling, Mary asked him privately, "Could you stop the Romans?"

Jesus, who was escaping the noonday sun under the shade of a twisted olive tree, looked quizzical. "Didn't you listen?"

Mary nodded. "You said that it was God's choice. Doesn't God act through you? Then it becomes your choice."

Jesus turned away without reply, but that afternoon he led her across the fields to a thicker part of the woods. They hacked through underbrush, which suddenly opened onto a clearing.

"I saw a boy do a miracle here. It satisfied what everyone wanted. It didn't mater if the miracle was true or not."

Jesus seemed to search around, then he found something. At first Mary couldn't tell what it was. He took what appeared to be a fallen stick and lifted it up—wrapped around it was a dead black adder, its head crushed.

"The miracle left this behind," he said. "The people were tricked, and then the tricksters killed this creature to hide their deception."

What was she supposed to understand from this? "You're not like that," said Mary.

"Unless I'm the snake," Jesus said, bluntly staring down at the dead reptile.

When she followed his gaze, Mary fell to her knees. The snake, its head a pulp of crushed bones and dried blood, was crawling up the stick toward Jesus's hand. It quivered, and its destroyed head regained its former shape. A flickering tongue shot out. The snake hissed, and Jesus dropped the stick, letting the adder make its escape through the grass. Mary felt her heart pounding.

"The Adversary," she whispered.

Was it really the Devil's work? Jesus didn't reply. But clearly his own lesson had been turned against him. Something beyond death was reaching out to him.

Several days passed in a blur. Jesus kept to himself wandering the hills. Mary made camp and left food and water out for him. She never saw Jesus take any, but when she woke up in the morning, the plate and jug were empty.

Finally he reappeared, kicking at the stones around the campfire, stamping out the flames. With one word Jesus wanted them to set off again: "Judas."

Several times before the trouble began, Mary thought she had spied him on the fringe of the crowds that constantly followed Jesus through the streets. But the man always kept his hood up and took care never to be standing anywhere near Mary. Once they started asking around, however, Judas's name was well known in the streets.

"Judas wants recruits. That's why he's not being as cautious as the Zealots," Jesus offered. He had no doubt who was leading the kanai and fomenting the local assassinations.

In less than a day the street urchins, fountains of all knowledge about the underground, led Jesus and Mary to the edge of town farthest from the Roman garrison and pointed to a cluster of outbuildings. What looked like a ramshackle barn surrounded by sheep pens had a door in the back. Jesus knocked, and Judas himself answered.

"You've come," he said, registering no surprise. He let them in, keeping his gaze on Mary and away from Jesus.

The back of the barn was floored and fitted out like a house. Sitting in a circle was a group of young men. Alarmed, a couple of them reached for their sheathed weapons. Judas said, "It's safe," and everyone waited for what came next.

"Are they holding you captive?" Jesus asked. The irony in his voice took Judas aback.

"They're loyalists," he said sharply. "Willing to die for God. Didn't that bring you here too?"

Jesus smiled to himself, all but saying, *You didn't answer my question.* He took a seat on the floor outside the circle. Mary sat down behind him.

"Has violence worked so well at home that you bring it here?" asked Jesus.

Judas shrugged. "What choice do I have?"

"Ah, that's right. You tried miracles already."

"We tried them," Judas reminded him. "Only it seems that one of us has gotten better."

In Mary's eyes Judas hadn't changed. Since he was released from jail, his hair and beard were rougher, his cloak was torn and clumsily mended. Judas stared Jesus down but saved a darting, covetous glance for Mary as he spoke. "Join me. I've made a start, and I know you haven't lost your will. Now you need to prove that you can fight."

"What if I listen to you?" asked Jesus, shaking his head. "We'd both be captives then."

It was the second time he'd used the taunt, and Judas allowed a flicker of irritation to break his confident expression. "Our people are crying out for freedom. Whatever you say, you can't argue against that. The cowards and the rich will keep hiding. Is that the side you want to join? Or do you plan to lead them?"

"I've thought about that for several days," said Jesus quietly. "And you're right. I can't lead the cowardly and the rich."

Judas already had his mouth open to interrupt, but this sudden change of tone caught him off guard. "What are you saying?"

"I will follow you. That's why I've come."

A smile creased Judas's thin lips, at first of disbelief. His gaze flicked between Jesus and Mary. He could read the shock in her face. "You're serious," he said cautiously.

Jesus let his head bow slightly. "What the Father wills, I cannot resist."

Mary couldn't stand it any longer. "No!" she cried. She would have jumped to her feet, but Jesus turned and placed a hand on her shoulder.

"You're free," he said. "Decide on your own. I told you I was watched over. Do you believe you are?"

As gentle as his voice sounded, the words stunned Mary like a betrayal. She had assumed that he would take care of her, that she was under his protection. Jesus read her thoughts. "I can't protect myself, so how can I protect you?"

Mary was in consternation—the last thing she wanted was to have Judas overhear this. He seemed to relish the confusion. "I'll protect you. Stay. If Jesus won't beg you to, I will."

The young men in the circle weren't hiding their feelings, which contained suspicion of Jesus and delight that a woman had come to serve them. Judas's smile broadened. "Don't worry. I can hold them in check."

Mary wanted to weep. Her eyes kept going to the door and her mind to the possibility of running away. What else had she been doing for months, ever since the Romans left her bereft? She forced herself to lean close enough to whisper to Jesus, which made the young men laugh.

"What will happen to me?"

There was no pity in his eyes. "You'll be hurt much worse if I pretend that my road is easy."

He stood up and held his hand out to Judas. After a last hesitation, Judas seized it. He didn't understand this unexpected pact, but he knew that it wasn't safe to have Jesus as a rival.

"You'll be my second," Judas said. "No one here will question your authority once I give the word."

"Except one," said Jesus quietly.

Suspicion returned to Judas's face, but before he could say anything, Jesus said, "I told you I can't resist God's will. He brought me here because you aren't safe. The traitor who threatens your life is in your midst."

Jesus didn't wait for Judas's reaction. "I'll join you tomorrow after I have bathed and purified myself." He took Mary by the hand to leave. "The problem isn't that the Romans already know your schemes and have sent someone to defeat you. The problem is that you think it's me."

Judas couldn't help himself. "Is it?" he snarled.

Jesus shook his head. "All you have to fear from me is that I come in peace."

11

THE FIRST AND LAST

Jesus and Mary walked slowly away from Judas's hideout. Whatever commotion Jesus's parting words had caused, it was muffled by the building's thick mud walls.

"How can you bring peace to someone who doesn't want it?" Mary asked.

Jesus replied, "I don't know. My feet walk where they are guided. I speak words that aren't mine anymore."

It was strange to realize the truth of what he said. As a child Jesus had lagged behind his father on the road one day, lying under a tree to gaze at the sky dappled through it. Joseph didn't worry since he had only a quarter mile to go before he reached the next job. The boy fell into a doze, only to be awakened by shouting.

A small crowd stood in a clump in the middle of the road. The shouting came from its center, and once Jesus fully woke up, he made out words.

"Kneel before me, I command thee! I wield the thunder. I crush the mightiest works of kings with one breath. Be afraid!"

To Jesus's surprise, a few in the clump of bystanders fell to their knees. Over their heads he saw a man dressed in tatters, apparently the remains of a rabbi's garments. He wore a long black beard, and his head bobbed back and forth violently, so much so that Jesus wondered why the man's head didn't fly off his shoulders.

"Tell us your name, rabbi," someone in the crowd said.

The bobbing grew more furious. "Fool! To hear my name is to be consumed in the fire. Did I not say that unto Moses?"

A few more sentences like this and Jesus realized that the man was speaking as God. Curiosity made the boy get up and approach. The bobbing head turned in his direction. Jesus was repelled—he hadn't seen that the ranter's cheeks were pierced with nails and his hair matted with fresh cow dung.

For some reason the sight of Jesus created a disturbing change. The tattered rabbi fell down and began to eat the dust of the road. His words were no longer coherent. The crowd dispersed, except for the few who remained kneeling, waiting for God's next gnomic utterance.

The memory troubled Jesus now. How was he any different from that? He couldn't prove that God spoke through him any more than he could prove that God didn't speak through that pitiful wanderer.

Except.

He would have turned to Mary and revealed the miracle of the burning house. It was his one proof. But at that moment Judas's band of rebels burst into the street like the contents of an exploding cauldron. Jesus and Mary ducked out of sight to watch.

Some had pulled out their curved knives, others came to blows with fists. The clamor drew Judas out into the street.

He had lost control over his followers, and the whole group hurled insults and suspicious accusations at one another.

Judas plunged into the melee. "Lackeys, fools!" he shouted. "Run home to your mothers. I don't care." He brandished a knife at the closest of the brawlers, who backed off immediately. "I have no use for any of you."

Up and down the street curious onlookers filled the doorways. Still arguing, the young rebels ran away. Their voices faded, and soon the scene was silent again.

"Now there will be peace," said Jesus. "The hornets' nest had to be smoked out first."

He stepped out of the shadows so that Judas could see him. "Don't be furious. The Father has brought you a blessing in disguise." To Judas, Jesus's mild tone concealed a triumphant smirk. He couldn't see it in the dark, but the very idea roiled his anger.

"Why did you come here? To practice sabotage?" Judas shouted. "When the Romans close their nets, you won't be left out. Or did they pay you?"

Jesus ignored the taunt. "Did you find your traitor?"

"Go to hell! You made him up."

Jesus ignored this too. "I suppose they all cast suspicion on each other."

"What else?" Judas snapped.

"Then you were running a conspiracy of traitors. It was only a matter of time before one of them turned the others in. It's you who won't escape the Romans' net."

Hearing his words thrown back at him, the fuming Judas approached, his fists balled up. Jesus smiled. "Real warriors aren't as prudent as you. They'd use a knife, even with all these people watching."

Once the brawl ended, all the neighbors had gone back inside, except for the most curious, who raised their lanterns to see what Judas might do.

Jesus had no fear of Judas. He pushed his fist down and said, "It's time to choose, and you only have a few minutes."

Suddenly Judas realized the danger he was in. Some bystander up or down the street was being paid off at that moment. The Romans took street brawls seriously when every mud hut could be concealing a clutch of rebels. Judas looked nervously over his shoulder.

"Why are you wasting time on him?" Mary interrupted. "We need to save ourselves."

Jesus shook his head, keeping his gaze fixed on Judas. "Do we stay together or not? Decide."

Judas's body rocked back and forth with indecision. "She's right. What use are we to each other?"

"I was your first disciple," said Jesus. "Where you go, I go."

Judas found this unbelievable. "There's nothing to follow anymore. You saw them scatter. There's nothing left to undermine, if that's your game."

Jesus shook his head. "Be grateful that they deserted you. They left an empty place that God will fill if you let him."

Judas was too confounded to consider if this was a veiled taunt. Recklessly, he bolted. Without a word, he turned and ran in the direction of the fields and woods, leaving Jesus and Mary to follow.

But Mary wouldn't. "We can't go with him. It's crazy," she protested. For a long time she had the measure of Judas, and Jesus's loyalty to him made her angry and confused. Try as she might, his motives were unreadable.

Knowing it would be futile, Mary pleaded. "Give me one good reason why you, who are blessed, should follow a man like Judas?"

"I must. The Father wants me to. If that's his will, you're safe too."

Mary wanted to accept that Jesus followed God's will, but that was the problem, not the solution. A man moved by God alone was like a leaf blown before the wind or a bird zigzagging from perch to perch. No plan, no direction could be seen.

As doubtful as Mary was, her fear of the Romans overrode everything else. They began to run. Their fleeing sandals slapped sharply against the stones. Echoes amplified the sound, as if their pursuers were already closing in. It wasn't safe to duck into a house along the way. Jesus's status as wonder-worker wasn't secure enough yet.

They met Judas on the edge of town. The moon provided their only light, but Jesus's skill at following trails in the dark hadn't faded. After a while the runaways found the camp Mary had made the night before. The banked fire still held a glow under its thick blanket of ash. The three could warm themselves and eat before bedding down among the olive trees.

They broke bread in silence. To the eye, nothing had changed from their days on the road. The previous days could have been a dream—there was no sign of an arrest or jail or miracles. Three wanderers sat out under the eternal stars, each lost in private thoughts.

After Mary had drawn some distance away to wrap herself in a blanket and sleep, Judas said, "I know you. You're not cunning or malicious. You don't have the mind for devious schemes. What do you want?"

"Haven't you asked that question every time we've met?" said Jesus. "Maybe the answer hasn't been revealed to either of us."

Judas hunched his shoulders against the cold. He kicked at the embers to extract some licks of flame. "I need a better answer than that."

Jesus put his hand out and touched Judas's shoulder. "From the moment we met, you have been the leader. I accept that. The Father speaks to me, and he tells me to follow you. Not for my own good, but for yours."

Judas jumped to his feet in agitation. "See? That's what you always do. You make meek speeches, but you're after me somehow. I'd rather be damned on my own than saved by you."

"Even if God has chosen us for miracles?"

"Us?"

"When he sends rain, it falls on everyone the same. Maybe this is the great time for all his people. You won't find out unless you step forward to receive with an open heart."

Before Judas could reply, Jesus held the palm of one hand over the fire. Instantly it sprang to life, as if a new log had been thrown on it. Judas stared, transfixed.

"God speaks in mysterious ways," said Jesus in a low voice. "Look closer."

Judas didn't need to be ordered—his eyes widened as the flames flickered, seeming to reach toward him. Suddenly Judas fell to his knees, putting his face so close to the flames that his complexion glowed red and sweaty. He stayed this way for a long time, long enough that for days afterward his face resembled the scalded hands of a washerwoman.

When the fire finally died away, Judas couldn't speak. His whole body had seemingly dissolved. After some time had passed, he managed to croak two words. "It spoke." Jesus nodded and waited. They both sensed that the next thing Judas said would be critical, perhaps fatal.

"It said that God would give me greatness if I repented."

Jesus was gentle, as if handling a frightened child. "Did it tell you how to repent?"

Judas shook his head. "Something I couldn't understand. The first and the last."

"Good."

Judas looked at him with bafflement. "You know what that means?"

"It means being first in this world is like being last in God's. We've both struggled to be first. I'm as guilty as you. Now we've been shown the way out. Become last on purpose. Surrender. How can we discover God's will unless we give up our own?" Jesus got to his feet, being careful not to touch Judas, who couldn't stop trembling. "It's cold. You ran away without your cloak."

Jesus took off the white robe he had been wearing and draped it around Judas's shoulders.

"How will you keep warm?" asked Judas. He sounded weak and embarrassed, but he knew he needed the cloak if he wasn't to freeze.

"Don't worry. I'm provided for," Jesus said. "I seem to have no control over that." He walked away and soon vanished in the darkness.

Whatever Jesus meant, Judas didn't ask. He was beginning to lose the uncontrollable tremor that all but rattled his bones. The fire had been a sign from God, but this wasn't the strangest thing. The strangest thing was that God knew him now, down to his marrow. He had been stripped clean by the fire; there was no escaping God's sight from this moment on.

Judas felt a wave of revulsion and humiliation. If God knew everything about him, did that mean Jesus did too? The possibility caused his mind to turn cold. Judas wrapped himself up beside the fire and tried to sleep. He lost consciousness almost immediately, but sat up with a start an hour later, staring groggily at the rising sliver of the moon. It wasn't the light that woke him up, however, but a sound.

A stranger was lurking nearby. Judas was about to call out, "Who goes there?" when he saw something. A shadowy silhouette just beyond the reach of the feeble campfire. And then something else, the silhouette's eyes, which glowed red in the dark.

As fear paralyzed Judas, the silhouette didn't approach, but sat down on the ground, the glowing eyes fixed on him. The demon—for what else could it be?—said, "Jesus does know you. Nothing escapes him."

Judas's jaw was locked, but after a moment his terror abated slightly. "Who are you?" he asked in a hoarse croak. "What do you want?"

"I want to glorify you. Jesus would have you surrender to God. Don't be a fool. Surrender is defeat."

The demon was echoing the doubts Judas spoke only to himself. "The fire told me I would be saved," he said.

The demon replied, "The fire has no power to decide. Your instinct is to fight. Who has the right to make you change? You choose. You decide."

Judas wanted to cry out that he chose salvation. But his heart was writhing. A war had started inside. He moaned, curling up into a tight ball.

Go away, he begged silently. *Go away.*

Nothing happened. In the darkness and silence, night creatures scurried back to their meal of worms and insects. The rising moon gave off a faintest glimmer, just enough to show Judas that he was alone. He had heard two voices in one night, one of hope, one of terror. That Judas couldn't tell them apart felt like his curse.

WITH THE DAWN something mystifying started to happen. Jesus became more contented and Judas more disgruntled. Having no more rivalry between them didn't satisfy Judas's soul. It was decided, by him alone, that they would wander around the Dead Sea until they found a safe village. It was too dangerous to return to where his band of rebels had been, and staying outside in the wilderness would only lead to exhaustion and starvation.

"If you're a true disciple, you'll show me how you do your miracles," said Judas. "God won't permit the servant to prosper and not the master."

"If it's God's will," Jesus said, directing his eyes toward the ground like a servant.

Judas snorted. "Keep it up. If you don't show me your miracles, either you're a fraud or you're lying about following me. Time will tell."

As they wandered Judas made Jesus do all the work, piling his back with their clothes and supplies, barking at him to find firewood every night and fetch water from hidden springs in the desert that took hours to find. The minute Jesus got back with pots of water on his shoulders, Judas set him to cooking supper. *He's turned him into a woman,* Mary thought. Most of this work had once fallen to her, but now Judas forced her to stand by, doing nothing as Jesus carried out every order without protest, no matter how petty. This show of meekness somehow made Judas boil inside.

One morning she caught Jesus alone when Judas left camp to scout the next village. His parting gesture was to kick the ashes of the fire in Jesus's face, accusing him of letting it die overnight. She said, "Why are you smiling? He's turning you into his slave girl."

"Should I be miserable instead?" replied Jesus. "If doing women's work was the way to despair, half the world would be despairing." He was kneeling in the dirt tying up their few thin blankets and making a pack out of the pots and vessels they carried with them from campsite to campsite.

In frustration Mary knocked the pots out of his hand. "Tell me what this is about or I'll run away. I'd rather be a whore again than watch him do this to you," she cried.

Jesus silently retrieved the scattered clay pots, one of which had broken when it struck a rock. He stared at the splintered shards. "You shall break them with a rod of iron, and dash them in pieces like a potter's vessel."

"Stop mumbling," Mary grumbled. Feeling her rage drain out of her, she collapsed on the ground beside him.

"I wasn't mumbling. I was explaining, the way you wanted. Do you recognize what I said?"

Mary lifted her chin. "I know some things. Not as much as a man." She quoted from the same psalm. "Serve the Lord with fear, with trembling kiss his feet." She shook her head. "Is that what you're doing? Serving Judas out of fear?"

"Haven't the Jews served the Lord that way, generation after generation, and what good has it done? More suffering, more punishment. We are the children of fear, except when a disaster strikes, and then fear turns into terror."

"But you were given the power to change that. All you have to do is touch someone. I've seen it." Mary wanted to take Jesus's hands to underline her words, but she didn't dare. He had become too different from any man she had ever known.

"If I use my power, people will become afraid of me too. And why not, if they fear my Father so greatly?"

By now Jesus had gathered everything they needed to move on that day. He sat down on the bundle of blankets and regarded her. "There is only one alternative to serving God out of fear. Serve him out of love. If I am to learn how to do that, what good is it to pick someone I already love, like you?"

Mary drank in those words. She hid her exhilaration behind a question. "So you chose someone hateful?"

Jesus smiled. "Judas isn't hateful. His mother found love in her heart for him."

"You're not his mother. Look at him. Every day he treats you worse."

"I wouldn't need faith if he treated me well, would I?" Jesus picked up a speck lying in the dust between his feet. "Can you tell what this is?"

Mary shook her head. She was in no mood for a lesson, but she knew that berating him anymore was pointless.

"It's a seed," said Jesus. "Of what I'm not sure. It could be mustard or a fig. They look alike, both tiny black specks." He tossed the seed into the scrub brush a few feet away. "That seed may fall on a rock or hard ground too barren to let it sprout. But nothing is certain. We could come this way years from now, and in the middle of a field of weeds there could be a magnificent fig tree. What is a speck today could feed a whole family tomorrow.

"I am that seed, and God has cast me among the weeds. But he didn't lose sight of me. I will fall on hard ground, or I will feed the multitudes. Let God decide."

"And that's your reason for taking Judas's abuse?" Mary sounded less bitter, but only slightly.

"Yes. If God is worth revering, it's out of fear or out of love. I can't live being afraid of my own Father. I choose love."

When Judas reappeared, he announced that the next village was safe. Jesus was loaded down, and they made their way to the place. The day had turned hot, as it did in the south even in early spring. Not a word was shared on the road until they passed fellow travelers on the narrow desert path.

Judas rebuked Jesus for looking away as the strangers approached. "Let them see you. I want to know if they recognize their savior."

None of the travelers recognized Jesus.

The next village resembled all the others they had passed through, equally full of dismal poverty and hollow-eyed denizens hanging around the streets like actors waiting for a drama that never began. Beggar boys followed the strangers with gaping curiosity. Judas ignored them all. He had his eye out for something, or someone, else.

When he spied an old mendicant slumped against a wall, he snatched the pack roughly from Jesus's back. "Come on, then."

He pulled Jesus by the collar of his cloak which was coarse, brown, and a size too big for him. Judas had kept the white one and thrown his old cloak over Jesus's shoulders.

The mendicant heard footsteps; he looked up warily, not sure whether to hold out his hand or hunch down in case the two strangers rained kicks and blows on him.

"Good masters," he whined.

"What can be good when I see you thus afflicted?" said Judas, raising his voice enough to be heard up and down the street.

"It's true, I have been sick. Alms, sir?"

The mendicant felt brave enough to take off his wool cap and hold it out. "Give bread to the poor and you give it to God."

Judas crouched down beside the beggar, who looked disappointed when he didn't hear the jingle of coins. Judas gave a curt nod, and Jesus crouched on the other side. "Take his hand," he ordered.

Jesus obeyed, taking the mendicant's right hand while Judas clasped the left.

The old man grew alarmed. "What are you doing?" He would have cried out, but arthritis had weakened and wasted him, and he had endured too many fevers. His shriveled hands fluttered like fallen birds in the strangers' grasp.

Jesus said, "There's nothing to fear, old one."

"What good is your pity?" Judas asked with sudden harshness. "God has shown me this poor man for us to heal. Grip his hand tighter. I will pray. We can do this together."

He glared with gimlet eyes at Jesus, who realized now why Judas was pleased that nobody recognized him on the road. This village was a clear field, a fresh start. If Jesus let Judas take the credit for a healing, the clamor would center on him.

"Ready?" said Judas. He made no effort to hide that this was a test. His mouth curled up at the corners as he squeezed the afflicted man's hand. It was a wonder his gnarled finger joints didn't turn to powder. "I have brought my most beloved disciple to you. Fear not."

The mendicant's eyes widened with anticipation. He began to mumble an incoherent prayer scraped together from half-remembered verses. Judas also prayed; his words were loud and clear. "Lord, you alone have the power to heal this, your son. Send me the gift of healing, not for my sake, but to pass it on to one in need."

Passersby began to take notice of the spectacle. Judas didn't open his eyes to see what Jesus was doing. "Do you feel it, little father? Do you feel the power?" he asked. A few bystanders began to murmur, watching and wondering.

The old mendicant trembled. "Yes," he whispered huskily. "I feel—something."

Mary was hanging back, half hidden in a doorway several yards down the street. She saw Jesus let go of the old man's hand. He got to his feet and looked around. Spotting Mary, he gestured for her to come, but he didn't wait. She caught up as he was rounding the next corner. She had grabbed up their bundled possessions from the street.

"I knew you wouldn't heal him. How could you? It was a trick," she said.

"That's not it," Jesus replied calmly. He didn't glance behind to see what Judas was doing. "He can order me all he wants. Ordering God is a bit more difficult." Jesus smiled. "Now that he has a crowd, I wonder how he'll get out of there."

"He'll talk his way out. That's my guess."

"Or God might fool all of us and heal the man. Imagine. Judas might even believe then. If his heart holds out."

Jesus was in very good humor. He took the bundles from Mary and put them over his shoulder again. Up ahead they could see a sign—a white dove scratched in chalk on a rough board, holding an olive branch in its beak. "We'll stop at the inn. Judas will find us when it's over."

Which he did. The crowd evidently hadn't torn Judas to pieces. Finding Jesus and Mary on a bench in a far corner of the inn, he marched up, towering over them.

"Give me one reason why I shouldn't kill you here and now." Judas's face was pale with fury.

"I gave you your miracle. You got away," said Jesus.

"I got lucky. The old fool was a crook. He was faking his afflictions, and when the crowd grew ugly, he threw his hands up, bawling to high heaven that I had healed him. He wanted to get out of there."

"Just like you," said Mary. Her jibe didn't divert Judas's focus from Jesus, who looked smaller than usual as he sat on the low bench beneath Judas.

"Maybe you did heal him. Maybe God secretly saved a man," Jesus said, not meeting Judas's glare.

"Don't be ridiculous!"

Suddenly a voice called out. "Judas!" A short man, his head hooded, came up. From Judas's expression it was obvious that he was one of his scattered followers. Judas wasn't pleased.

"How did you find me, Micah?" he growled.

"Never mind. The question is, why you haven't found us?" The man called Micah threw back his hood. He was older than the hotheaded young men who were in Judas's band. His face was swarthy, with a scar at the hairline.

Judas evaded the question. "Have the Zealots penetrated this far?" he asked.

Micah nodded. "We even have a capture. Come. And bring your friends. You've attracted too much attention already."

They got up to follow the conspirator into a back room. Mary found herself light-headed. "Steady," Jesus whispered, taking her hand.

Past the back room and down a corridor, Micah showed the way into the cellar. As they descended the stairs, their eyes adjusted to a pair of smoking torches in the hands of two men. Startled, the two grabbed for their weapons.

Micah held his hand up. He was apparently the chief, because the two guards obeyed immediately. He turned to Judas.

"I have news from Simon. We were worried about you," he said. "Then we got word from Jerusalem. You failed in your mission. Simon was disappointed. Very disappointed."

Jesus glanced at Judas, who revealed no emotion. Under any ordinary circumstance Micah's veiled threat would have been a death sentence. But Judas had his eyes fixed on something. A blindfolded man was bound hand and foot, his body stretched out on a table in the dark cellar. Streaks of dried blood told that he had been tortured.

Now the sound of voices caused him to emit a muffled moan. He tried to speak, but only garbled sounds came out.

One of the guards approached. "If you'd told us what we wanted to know, you'd still have a tongue," he said. He slapped the blindfolded man with the back of his hand.

The victim, who had raised his head, let it slump back onto the table again. He went silent, probably from passing out. Traces of military garb were left on his torso, with an insignia.

"An officer. You got yourself an officer," Judas said. He looked at Micah, seemingly unafraid. But Jesus sensed that Micah was the worst of the worst. His fanaticism meant more than life to him.

Judas inquired, "Why didn't you ransom him?"

"He's a special envoy from the proconsul, Pontius Pilate. They know his name in Rome. Next month they'll find his head in an alley. We have to make them afraid, not just our own priests and Jewish collaborators."

The two guards grunted their approval of Micah's tactic. Their leader smiled faintly. "But there's still leftover business, isn't there, Judas?" he said. "You failed." He edged closer to Judas until he was almost in his face.

"Not me. This one." Judas indicated Jesus. At this, Mary started to cry out, but Jesus seized her arm and squeezed it just in time.

Judas continued. "You, Micah, weren't in the council. Simon sent me to test the courage of a new recruit. When the time came, he couldn't go through with it."

Micah looked suspicious. "Why didn't you get rid of him? Better dead than a coward."

"I'm too soft-hearted," said Judas. "I felt the impulse to give him a second chance. I shouldn't have." Even with the threat of death hanging over him, Judas kept his cool demeanor. "He begged for his life, and I told him he would face one more test."

Judas pulled out his knife and held it up. "Let him kill your Roman. You've done well. Your captive is ready to die."

Micah looked skeptical, but Judas turned quickly to Jesus, pressing the knife into his hand. "Go ahead. Kill the enemy. It won't make amends for failing, but at least we'll know how loyal you really are."

Jesus drew his hand away, but Judas folded it tighter over the knife. "You claimed that God came to help me today. Let's see if he helps you."

Jesus met Judas's gaze steadily. "He will."

Micah shook his head. "It's not much to finish off the half-dead already." For the first time Judas blanched. He would have tried a more desperate strategy, but Micah had more to say.

"On the other hand, the alternative is for me to kill your new recruit." He directed a leer at Mary. "And since your lovely companion knows everything now, she would have to be eradicated with him. Do you know what I call that, Judas?"

Judas shook his head.

"Messy. I have one corpse to sneak out of here. Two more is simply messy."

Judas didn't reply. He and Jesus and Mary were in the hands of a sadist. Micah was in total control, and they were helpless to do anything but let him play out his nasty game.

Micah approached Jesus. "All right. Kill him. It won't be a true test of loyalty. Let's consider it probation." He brandished his own knife. "Of course, not everyone passes probation."

The bloody prisoner moaned again. His body strained against its bonds—he knew what was coming. Jesus stepped closer. He held the point of the knife directly over the Roman's heart.

Mary cried out. "No!"

"What would you have me do, resist this evil?" asked Jesus.

"Yes, you have to. We can die together."

Mary was sobbing now. The conspirators stood ready to rush at her. Jesus kept speaking as if they were the only two people in the room. "If God had wanted to destroy evil, he would have brought the world to an end. He didn't. He offered us a covenant of peace instead."

No one knows what would have happened next, except that suddenly the dying Roman officer sat up and raised his arms. Micah later swore that Jesus had cut his ropes in the dark cellar, even though no one saw him do it. However the soldier got free, he opened his eyes and stared at Jesus, transfixed.

"I am ready," he croaked. Even though he was tongueless, the words were clear. The assassins were amazed and always insisted on this detail afterward.

Jesus placed his hand on the prisoner's head. "The Father's mercy be on you," he said in a low voice.

Tears streamed down the prisoner's face. "What Father?" he asked.

"The one who sent you here and now brings you home."

Jesus put the knife in the prisoner's hands, gently so that the blade wouldn't cut him. He placed it with the hilt upward. For all the world it looked like one of the crosses that the Romans tied condemned Jewish rebels to when they wanted to make a public display of their deaths. The prisoner, who had seen more than his share of crucifixions, stared blankly at the knife.

"Why?" he mumbled.

"Because the tormented and the tormentor are equal in God's eyes," said Jesus. The words weren't his. They came through him, and like the prisoner he shuddered at the cross made by the knife.

In his half-crazed state, the prisoner thought he was being offered the noble way out. His hands trembled as he turned the point toward his heart. The Zealots remained frozen in place, waiting for the suicide to come.

"No," said Jesus, pulling the weapon away from the prisoner's chest. "You are called."

He held up his hand, and the prisoner gave a loud gasp that rattled in his throat. He slumped over; the knife fell from his hand, clattering on the floor.

"There," Jesus said. "It is done."

No one opposed him as he walked over to Mary and took her by the hand. They headed toward the narrow staircase that led back to the inn. Judas blocked the way.

"You send a Roman to Heaven?" he shouted. "You're no messiah. You're a madman."

Suddenly the three Zealots came to life. "Messiah?" Micah echoed. He stared at Judas. Maybe he had two madmen on his hands.

Jesus shook his head. "God has shown mercy to someone you condemned. That leaves you with a terrible possibility. Maybe the messiah has come, but he's here to save Romans too."

The words were blasphemous, stunning the Zealots. For a quick moment they couldn't move. Jesus pushed Judas aside. Holding Mary's hand, he led her upstairs. The noise of drunken revels could be heard overhead. They almost crashed into a wine cask at the top of the stairs and the next moment were gone.

PART THREE

MESSIAH

12

PURE IN SPIRIT

As they reentered the raucous inn, Jesus could sense Mary's shock at the prisoner's death. She trembled at the prospect of being set upon before they could make an escape.

"No one saw us go downstairs," Jesus said, keeping his voice calm and level. "We have to leave by the front. Just put one foot in front of the other, slowly." He held on to Mary's arm. "The Zealots can't run after us. They know what will happen if they get caught with a dead Roman."

Heads turned as the two walked through the dark, smoke-filled outer room. Smoke fumed out from a corner fireplace where haunches of goat meat were roasting. The greasy haze made the drunkards' faces look sinister.

But nobody lifted a hand to stop them, and a moment later they were outside. The bright sunlight didn't come as a relief to Mary—she almost doubled over from the quaking in her abdomen. Across the lane Jesus saw a wide doorway floored with paving stone instead of dirt, a sign that a well-off merchant lived there. He led Mary over to it, and she collapsed.

For a long time there was nothing to do but hold her. They attracted little attention—people were used to small scenes of misery on the streets. When he thought she had calmed down, Jesus said gently, "Have you ever seen anyone die before?"

Mary shook her head. "Not like that." She drew in a ragged breath.

Jesus looked away. Tending to her had given him a few moments in which he could forget himself. Now he felt a rush of hopelessness. In his mind he had been following God's will. But God didn't run, and that was all he had been doing since that first night he entered the Zealots' cave.

"I feel lost," Jesus muttered. "God's mercy went to a Gentile who hates and persecutes the Jews. But I've been shown no mercy, so what does that make me?"

"Don't." Mary embraced him more desperately. "Doubt will destroy us both."

Jesus remembered the knife blade gripped in the dying Roman soldier's hands and the uncanny way it resembled a cross. It wasn't failure that was causing his despair, but a premonition of something unthinkable. An act no loving father would permit.

Suddenly Mary's embrace felt suffocating. Whatever trials God had in mind for him, Jesus had to face them alone. He freed himself from her arms and stood up. "You're not safe with me. I'm going to find a way for you to get back to Jerusalem."

Mary could have pleaded for him not to abandon her. She knew very well that her part so far had been to weep and run away. The thought shamed her and made her feel exhausted. She pulled her head cloth over her face. Curious passersby were beginning to take notice. Jesus crouched back down and faced her. "I've brought you nothing except disaster. We should still have faith. What else can save us?"

Mary had one answer left, a secret one she had been suppressing too long. She lifted her head, her eyes burning into Jesus's, and she began to kiss him. His surprise and the force of her passion pushed him back, almost knocking him off balance.

"Love me," she pleaded, her words hardly distinguishable from a moan. She pressed her lips to his again.

Jesus felt the rush of arousal. He had never kissed a woman this way in his life. He didn't pull back. There was nothing more to lose; he couldn't posture as being too holy and pure. He felt Mary waiting. She wasn't so lost in passion that her instincts were gone. She would know in the next instant whether she had any hope with Jesus as a lover. Faith was nothing if not faith in him.

We make a mistake about God when we think that his infinity is somehow larger than the universe. Infinity is larger than the largest, but also smaller than the smallest. Divine intervention can happen in a split second, inserting itself between one breath and the next. Between a kiss and a response.

The arousal rising in Jesus's body reached his heart, where it did something unexpected—it turned from passion into light. His heart became filled with a white radiance. It didn't extinguish his love for Mary. It exploded instead, smashing all boundaries. Jesus felt overwhelmed by a wave of bliss that enveloped everything around him. Mary gasped, and he knew that the same mystery engulfed her.

You are my most beloved.

The words came from the same source that drew him into the burning house. This time it enveloped them both.

Jesus felt immense relief. The law of Moses commands every man to marry. He had suffered over this, but now he saw that he would fulfill the law in a different way, by marrying through God.

Jesus looked into Mary's eyes. Had she heard the words? Had she felt light filling her body, dissolving it, as if the body suddenly became spirit? Mary's gaze melted, losing every trace of despair. She pulled back and would have spoken, but another event intervened.

A man's shadow fell over them. It was felt before it was seen, a coolness that shielded the sun. At that moment Jesus was torn. He wanted to cling to Mary in their shared bliss, a spell he would have sacrificed anything to keep from breaking. But the man's shadow meant something fateful. Jesus knew it instantly. The stranger spoke, his face still silhouetted against the sunlight.

"Master."

Jesus thought of the first person who had ever called him that. Had Querulus managed to find him? He let go of Mary, who remained crouching in the doorway, and began to rise. The stranger bent down to help him to his feet, and now Jesus could see that the face was darker and thicker than the aristocratic old Roman's.

This didn't prevent Jesus from giving the same reply he gave to Querulus that first night. "I am no one's master," he mumbled.

"Or everyone's."

The man, once he could be viewed closely, was a Jew dressed in the same kind of white cloak that Querulus had given Jesus. He was sober in tone, almost solemn, with eyes that could not tear themselves away from Jesus.

"You are above anything I can understand, yet you are everything I've ever wanted. I can't imagine it." The stranger sounded abashed and hesitant, as if he had practiced this speech a hundred times, only to find that it didn't remotely fit the moment. Jesus drew back, and the stranger quickly added, "I know I haven't made a mistake. Come."

Jesus allowed himself to be helped up, but he pushed away the stranger's hands, which were large and rough, as they reached out for his. Before he could turn back to Mary, the stranger lifted her up too. She had gone limp, and it was like lifting a deadweight.

"Why should I come with you?" Jesus was certain that one of the watchers had come out of the shadows to find him, as Querulus predicted would happen.

The stranger replied, "I am a messenger sent to you, but you are a messenger sent to the world. Have you heard of us?"

"Yes."

"Then you know that we've been aware of you for a long time."

"How?" Jesus's tone was wary.

"First by signs and divinations. The stars told us part of the story; so did the prophets. God told us the rest."

"You shouldn't trust in signs, and the prophets spoke hundreds of years ago."

"I know." The reticence of Jesus's replies didn't stop the stranger, whose emotions, once released, kept rising. "It's beyond anything I could imagine that I've found you. I came alone, but my whole community has prayed for this moment."

"I'm sorry. You've deluded yourself."

The stranger stepped back, startled. "You can't mean that."

"Why not? Do you think you're the only Jew who hasn't found the messiah?" The last trace of bliss had gone; there was no radiance left in his heart. "I know what it means to be deluded."

Mary had recovered enough to feel embarrassment at the intimate scene the stranger had intruded upon. She smoothed her robe and tried to comb out the tangles in her hair with her fingers. "Let's go," she whispered to Jesus.

The stranger overheard her. "No, you mustn't."

He blocked the way, his eyes anxiously searching Jesus's face. "Don't you understand, you of all people? Yours isn't the path of joy. 'He was despised and forsaken of men. A man of sorrows and acquainted with grief.'"

All three of them knew the words of Isaiah the prophet. Jesus resisted their meaning. "Being despised doesn't make me chosen. Let us pass." He waited. He wouldn't push the stranger aside, not for a few more seconds.

Biting his lip, the stranger held his ground. "I never expected it to be like this," he muttered, searching for words of persuasion that didn't come. He had no choice but to let them pass. Jesus took Mary's hand to reassure her; they stepped back into the street.

They had only walked a few yards when the stranger's voice reached them again. "You're afraid to die. Just like the rest of us."

Jesus turned his head, his gaze steady. "Yes."

"So afraid that you'd condemn the rest of us to death? So afraid that you'd make all our prophets into liars?"

Mary felt Jesus hesitate; she tightened her grip on his arm. "Don't listen. We can't go back."

Jesus tried to obey her. He kept walking, but the watcher's taunts dogged them.

"Should Jerusalem crumble because you tremble? Tell me. The others will want to know. Show us what fools we were to believe. Would that satisfy you?"

The stranger kept pace behind them, shouting. Then Jesus felt Mary let go of his hand. "You believe him?"

Jesus glanced at her. Without her speaking, her eyes said, *You're already gone. We both know it.*

Jesus reached out to find her hand again, but he was too late. Mary ran. She gathered up the bottom of her cloak so that it wouldn't slow her down. Her bare legs made her look like a pale gazelle in the desert fleeing a prowling lion. Behind him the stranger kept silent, watching until Mary disappeared around a narrow, winding corner. He had coaxed and goaded Jesus into his net, but for the moment his hold was so fragile it might break at the touch.

THE MESSENGER'S NAME, it turned out, was Tobias. He brought two mounts with him, a good strong horse with a saddle and a donkey tethered behind it loaded with bags of food and various goods—apparently the stranger sold these along his route.

"I wandered a long time to find you," he said. "I had to support myself."

Jesus was given his choice of beast to ride. He had never seen a Jew on horseback, only Romans, much less did he know what to do in the saddle. He climbed on the back of the donkey, straddling the bags on either side. On the road the sight of the two companions made other travelers smile—one man erect on a groomed and muscled horse, the other hunched on a swaybacked donkey that drifted to the side of the road whenever it spotted a promising tuft of new spring grass.

Neither spoke. They were lost in different moods of silence. Jesus's thoughts kept returning to Mary and the sensation of her hand jerking away from his. Tobias couldn't wrap his mind around the idea that age-old prophecies had come true. As they sat around the fire on the first night, Jesus broke the silence.

"Is the messiah a man?" he asked, staring into the flames. "Or can he disobey the law without being punished?"

"What?" Tobias couldn't have been more startled.

"If he is a man," said Jesus, "he must marry. That's the law of our fathers. But what if God won't let him?"

Tobias was at a loss to reply. Jesus spoke low and turned his gaze on his companion. "What do you say? Have the watchers learned anything in all their years of praying?"

Tobias hesitated. "What the messiah says and does can only be known by him."

"So he isn't a man. I have never satisfied a woman. They're a mystery to me. I'm a mystery to myself. Is that what your people want, someone more confused than they are?"

Tobias jumped to his feet, looking afraid. "How can you ask me such things?"

"I don't really know."

Jesus said these words simply, but they made the watcher more nervous. He paced back and forth, the flickering fire turning him into a phantom of glowing orange that rippled with black shadows. "It's not fair to test me this way."

"Why not? You said you were certain you hadn't made a mistake."

"I am."

Jesus laughed. "You don't look like it. Sit down. Go ahead. I understand now."

It took some coaxing before Tobias would consent to return to the log that they had pulled up to the fire. He didn't want to talk; instead, he busied himself scraping the crockery plates, wiping them clean with a scrap of cloth, and stuffing them back into a saddlebag. After the fire had been banked and the two were rolled up in their sleeping blankets, Tobias asked, "What do you understand?"

"You don't want a messiah. You want an idol."

"That's not true." Tobias responded a touch too quickly. He knew the law prohibiting idols, had known it since he was four or five years old.

Jesus ignored his protest. "An idol can be worshiped on a shelf. It makes no trouble. It never has doubts, so you can trap God in the cage of your own fantasies. What could be better?"

Tobias rolled himself up tighter in his blanket and gave a muffled reply.

"What's that?" Jesus asked.

Tobias poked his head out. "I said I'm taking you back to the others. That's my mission. I don't have to understand you."

"I don't think you can avoid trying to understand me."

"We'll see."

Tobias satisfied himself with this clipped rebuttal; he stuck his head back into the wool cocoon. The next morning he acted sullen, rattling the pots and pans and breaking an eating bowl. He had little more to say when they were on the road again.

Jesus was unsettled too. He had made a glancing reference to Mary, genuinely wondering what Tobias thought. What were his duties as a man now that God had changed everything? Maybe those who had spent their lives praying for the messiah knew more about him than he did himself.

The terrain remained barren, rising into brown hills covered with withered grass. So it came as a surprise, on the following day, when the horse and donkey came over a rise and down below was spread a patchwork of green gardens. In the glaring sun their green was like an emerald flashing in the mud. The gardens were empty, and Jesus asked where Tobias's people were.

"We bathe before the noon meal and pray until two hours before sunset," Tobias had fallen into the habit of providing nothing but short, factual answers. As they wended down the switchbacks that led to the oasis, Jesus recognized that the sect he was about to meet could be no other than the Essenes. They were recluses, reputed to be the most secret sect in Judea. In Galilee Essenes were unknown. They could just as well be mythical. Where they lived, around the Dead Sea, the Essenes inhabited caves and hillside enclaves, rarely going to Jerusalem, even for High Holy Days.

The sight of home made Tobias sit taller in the saddle. "They'll know we're coming." Like the Zealots, the Essenes kept watch, and Jesus heard sharp whistling tones that were not quail or pheasants or any other bird. Were the Essenes as suspicious as the Zealots? As angry? The more pressing question was what would happen when Jesus appeared among them. Tobias answered before he could ask.

"A banquet is prepared before you."

"Doesn't that take time? We just came over the rise," said Jesus.

"What kind of watchers would we be if we had to use our eyes?" The Essenes had learned to be confident, if nothing else. At the first sight of home, Tobias seemed to lose his doubts about the prize he was bringing to his people.

As they approached the green gardens, figures began to appear. Scattered houses, made of finer stone and mortar than the mud dwellings of the villages they had passed, were concealed in the shade of a thick stand of pines. At first the Essenes looked ghostly, stepping into the sun in gleaming white robes, the same garment worn by men, women, and children.

"I had a robe like that," Jesus said.

"We know. It connected you to us. You'll have a new one after you bathe and rest." Tobias was as much the focus of attention as Jesus. The way he sat, erect and proud, signified that he had succeeded in his mission. To capture the messiah was like capturing an eagle with one's bare hands. People stared at Jesus with tears in their eyes. They would have shouted hallelujahs, Jesus thought, except that some ingrained sense of dignity prevented it. Mothers covered the faces of their youngest children with their skirts to keep excited cries from insulting their guest.

The trail ended at a large meeting house or synagogue. In front a line of elders waited, all of them with gray or even white beards. Before Jesus could dismount, each walked up and touched his feet. The last supplicant was the very oldest, who murmured, "May you never leave us."

Amen.

A hundred voices prayed this last word in unison, making a soft, unearthly hum in the air. Jesus turned around and saw the whole community standing behind him. Who were they? He didn't know yet, but they weren't like the others, the villagers who grew hysterical when they knew who he was, grabbing at him like carrion birds to tear off their scrap of flesh. The Essenes were all but silent, their heads half bowed.

Be glorified.

The new words also filled the air with an unearthly hum. Did they come from the Essenes or from above? Tobias led him into the gathering hall—the elders parted to make way, a sign of respect. As Jesus stepped inside, he saw a plain empty room with whitewashed walls and high windows. The interior felt like a synagogue, but there were no scrolls or altar. Except for low wooden benches arranged in rows, the entire space was devoted to paintings that filled the walls on all sides.

All the paintings were of him and his life, both past and future.

Tobias turned around, sensing that Jesus had stopped in his tracks: "Now you know why it wasn't impossible to find you."

Jesus barely heard what he said; his heart was pounding in his ears. He recognized scenes from his life in Nazareth: cutting stone with his father, sitting in a circle with his brothers and sisters while the rabbi read stories about the exodus from Egypt. But other images weren't recognizable. He was painted sitting on a throne among the clouds and riding a donkey into Jerusalem while people laid palm fronds down in front of him.

No one had followed them inside. They wanted Jesus to view this spectacle privately, to react without being spied upon.

"Where did these come from?" Jesus sounded hoarse, but his face betrayed little reaction.

"No one knows," Tobias replied. Jesus gave him a baffled stare. "The first one appeared when I was a child too small to remember it." He pointed to a painting in the far corner.

Jesus barely recognized Joseph and Mary, bundled in thick winter clothes. She was suckling a newborn baby, yet the surroundings didn't look like the home Jesus knew. It was more like a barn or stable. Vague outlines of cattle and sheep appeared in the background. His parents had never spoken about such a place.

"You're saying no human hand painted these?"

Tobias nodded. "Every winter on the shortest day of the year a new one appears. Our elders had a vision telling them to build this hall with bare white walls. Nothing else was revealed. Because we are Essenes, we obeyed. We have no other purpose in life. For many years the purpose of this place was a secret. We were told to keep the hall sealed, until one day another vision came. And we found this."

He pointed to one of the high windows, not to a painting. Jesus squinted against the sunbeams that poured through, flecked with luminous, dancing motes of dust. Just below the window some words could be made out in black Hebrew letters: *Light of the world.*

"The rest came very fast," Tobias said. When Jesus looked around, each window had its own words. *Messiah. Anointed One. Lamb of God. King of Kings.* Every Jew knew them as tokens from the prophets.

"So you see, the signs and divinations weren't hard to interpret. We'd have to be blind to miss them." Tobias was smiling this whole time. He took a small measure of enjoyment in surprising Jesus.

Jesus approached the painting that showed Mary and Joseph in the stable; he brushed his fingers lightly over the hem of her coarse wool robe. It was true to life. She had worn it every winter of his life.

"Your people are pure in spirit," said Jesus. "That's why these have come to you."

The pounding in his ears had ceased. Jesus swung his gaze around the hall, taking in every scene. One patch of wall was draped with a linen sheet, hiding the image behind it. "Why is that one covered up?"

Tobias shrugged. "It's the last one to appear. We came into the hall as always, on the shortest day of the year. But this time was different. The image didn't show the messiah."

"Who did it show? I want to see."

"Of course."

With some hesitation Tobias went over and tugged at the sheet, which fell from its hooks.

"We couldn't understand," he said. "It's not even finished."

The painting captured only a barren low hill under an overcast sky. It could have been any hill in Judea, and there was no reason it belonged among the other paintings. The invisible hand that made it had stopped short, although when Jesus walked closer, he could make out, just barely, the faint outline of something. Three crosses stood on the brow of the hill, barely sketched in.

"Were we right to cover it up?" asked Tobias.

Jesus's face had become pale. "Leave it exposed. I know why it's this way."

"Why?"

"It was left for me to finish."

13

TRAVELER

On the day Jesus announced that he was leaving, the word spread like wildfire. The Essenes had awaited his departure for five years. His purpose wasn't to stay. Wasn't it written that the savior would conquer Jerusalem and enter the Temple in triumph? It was also the day the Essenes would be personally vindicated. No one in the outside world cared about them. While every Jew prayed for the messiah, the Essenes were too extreme. They were so pure that they never married. They practiced celibacy to atone for the disobedience of Adam and Eve, and newcomers had to serve the sect for ten years before being accepted into the group.

Now at last the Essenes would be rewarded. In their minds, God knew every detail of their enormous sacrifice.

"We'll march to the Temple behind you," Tobias declared. "We're not fighters. We don't have weapons, but that won't matter, will it?" He envisioned Roman soldiers falling like rows of wheat in a field when Jesus raised his hand.

Jesus shook his head and said that he would go alone.

Tobias was concerned. "I know you won't fail," he stuttered. But no army at all? The messiah had been prophesied as a warrior. What else could he be? Violence was woven into the scriptures like a bloody thread, beginning with God's curse of the serpent and the mark of Cain in the book of Genesis. On down through the history of the Israelites, between God's punishments and the constant battles for survival, the world was filled with violence.

"Can I, at least, go with you?" Tobias asked.

"You're curious to see me bring down the Roman fortifications. By blowing the *shofar,* maybe?"

Tobias looked hopeful. "We have one. You can take it." Ever since the ram's horn brought victory at Jericho, centuries before, a shofar had been part of the High Holy Days.

Jesus put his hand on Tobias's shoulder. "You can come. Of everyone here, you deserve to. But I seek what cannot be sought. And when I find it, you will not see what it is. The wind is more visible."

Tobias smiled. "But one can feel the wind and go where it wants you to go."

Preparations happened quickly and with great excitement. A pack donkey was loaded and hitched to the back of a wagon. Jesus refused anything more elaborate, and when the elders hinted at some hidden caches of knives and armor, Jesus ignored them. Runners went higher into the hills to gather the other scattered Essenes who lived outside the center at Qumran. As they gathered at the high plateau where Qumran sat, a mile from the Dead Sea, the arrivals looked strangely pale for a desert people. But, then, many of the older men devoted their days to copying scripture, bent over candlelit tables in dark houses and caves. Even after half a day's journey they blinked in the sun like ruffled owls.

Jesus watched all things with an aloofness no one could explain. He came to the feast given in his honor, but he sat at the head table barely sipping a goblet of wine and absent-mindedly tearing at his bread. The next day he gathered as many in the assembly hall as could fit, filling the benches and crowding every square inch of the floor. It was noon in high summer; the air was barely breathable. He knew almost every face. Hadn't he lived among the Essenes for five years now? He had taught in every community, feasted with the rabbis, and argued the smallest scrap of the law and the *midrash*.

Jesus told them that the real scriptures were not in the scrolls of the Torah. "If God is everywhere, we must figure out why he's so hard to see," he once said when somebody found him crouched in a field studying something intently on the ground. It turned out to be a lark's nest hidden in the grass. A clutch of eggs had just hatched, and the blind fledglings in the nest mistook Jesus's shadow for the return of their mother. They opened their huge pink beaks, crying and weaving their heads for food.

Such somber moments were rare. Jesus brought more joy to the Essenes than they had ever known. He shocked the rabbis by declaring that God's creation was as pure as the day Eden appeared. For him, the Fall didn't exist. "Look at the birds of the air and the lilies of the field," he said. "Can you name a commandment that they break?" He taught that innocence was closeness to God and that all creatures were created innocent.

"Eve angered God, and our innocence was taken away," the rabbis insisted.

Jesus smiled. "Women have mysterious powers, but I doubt they could destroy what God created. We have only fallen in the mud, and mud can be washed off."

The rabbis weren't convinced; no one has the right to contradict the Torah. But ordinary people believed him and loved his teachings. On the outside Jesus was recognizably the same young man who first appeared in their midst, but God had worked tremendous changes inside, had fashioned a pillar of strength from a green sapling.

Now Jesus cast his eyes over the gathering, waiting for silence before he said, "Have I disappointed you? I must have. Otherwise, it is God who has failed, and that is impossible."

A confused buzz arose from the crowd. No one expected the talk to begin like this.

"I hear no reply," said Jesus. "If I have satisfied you, then you are all saved, right? The Jews are fulfilled. Is that what you want me to believe?"

Was this a test? Confusion spread; there were troubled outcries. "Master, tell us what you mean."

Jesus held his hand up for silence. "You want me to vanquish your enemies and return the land to God. I can't do anything until you answer me one question. Why do you need me? Why are you not saved already? Someone speak."

Tobias, sitting in the front row, felt his heart pounding. He would have jumped to his feet, but one of the elders stood up nearby.

The old man spoke haltingly, trying to hide his distress. "Master, the Jews cannot save themselves. The Romans hold our land by force; they tax us until we are beggared. Thousands of rebels have died, and their families have been murdered in retribution. You know all this."

Jesus nodded. "God knows all this too. So why has he stood by and done nothing?"

The elder cleared his throat. He had learned submission to the wisdom of their young master, but it was another thing to be quizzed like a dull schoolboy.

"God has waited until we atoned for our sins," he said. He swept his arm across the whole congregation. "Everyone here has joined in one great act of atonement. All our years of purity serve that end, to earn God's mercy."

Jesus frowned. "It doesn't seem that you've earned much mercy. What do you really have? Spinach mixed with dirt to eat, a few scrawny sheep half starved on desert scrub. Many sinners have been given more."

The crowd was stunned. The last thing they ever expected was to hear Jesus treat them with contempt. Yet whatever they heard, Jesus wasn't being scornful. Until a month ago he blended in with the Essenes. But one night, when he was walking late among the olive groves, something happened. It seemed like nothing at first. He looked up at the moon through the tangled branches of the oldest tree in the grove. The branches looked like a net, and the moon was a bright fish caught in it, ready to be dragged to shore.

Suddenly Jesus felt a pang in his heart. He kept staring; the image grew ominous, because he knew that the Essenes would fail. Their purity wouldn't save them. Like the moon, they were trapped. No tiny sect could atone for the past. Generations would pass, and the Jews would remain slaves. Their only hope was still a secret.

Jesus knew two things at that moment. He must leave to find the secret, and he could not allow the Essenes to follow him in case he failed.

He steeled himself again the dismay of his listeners. "God sees everything. Arrogance is hidden in meekness, and pride in purity," he said. "You are misguided to believe that you could totally cleanse yourselves, and the worst mistake you made was to believe that I can save Israel." Jesus ignored the waves of shock that were now turning into ones of anger. "I came as your friend," he said, raising his voice. "And I will not leave as your enemy. But if you expect me to shout down the walls of Jerusalem like Joshua before Jericho, you are deluded."

The Essene men jumped to their feet shouting; the women began to wail. Tobias was among the few who kept his place, bowing his head and praying that the master had some secret meaning in mind.

Jesus interjected. "What, now you turn on me, so quickly? A few words of rebuke, and your love turns to hate?"

Standing by an altar table piled high with gold ornaments and exotic fruits, placed in reverence to him, Jesus cleared the table, sending the metal bracelets and amulets clattering to the floor. Then, he leaped on top and spread his arms, shouting to be heard above the din. "Sit down! Calm yourselves!"

Many were too riled to listen to him, but the women and the cooler heads among the men coaxed them to sit down again. Jesus spoke above the angry muttering and oaths.

"I am not leaving for myself, but for you," Jesus said. "All you've ever wanted from me is to save the Jews. The Jews cannot be saved as long as the world is what it is. We need a new world, nothing less."

No one understood his meaning, but mixed into these words was still a faint hope, and so the crowd became less tense. Someone exclaimed, "How will you bring a new world, master?"

"I don't know. I only know that I cannot be what you imagined. I am no warrior against our oppressors." Jesus lowered his head. His meek tone stirred the audience, even as upset as they were.

Tobias rose to his feet, unable to keep silent any longer. "Others broke the covenant, not us. We've tried with all our hearts to honor God. We've obeyed his commandments, repented of every sin, no matter how small." There was a murmur of agreement in the hall.

Jesus replied slowly. "You are the purest people I've ever known. God loves you for it. But he will not save you for it."

"What are you saying, that no amount of goodness can satisfy him?"

Jesus shook his head. "God is more than goodness. God is a mystery."

"And you haven't solved it?"

"Not yet. But I am closer than the day I arrived."

The air was filled with a low moan. Tobias looked around. "You can't leave us in despair. We took you as our teacher. Teach us."

Jesus shook his head. "Let me go. Forget I was ever here." He jumped down from the table and made his way to the door. Women started to wail again; men slumped with their heads in their hands. A day that began in celebration had been scraped down to bone.

Tobias caught up with Jesus. "Look at what you're doing. Come back. We'll be hopeless."

"Be calm, Tobias. It's no one's fault." Despite the turmoil he had created, Jesus seemed as composed as ever. "Bring the wagon around. We leave immediately." Tobias set his jaw, refusing to budge. In a gentler voice Jesus said, "It's for the best. God can speak and still cause tears. You know that well enough."

If Tobias had a reaction, he turned away too fast for it to be seen. He walked into the pine grove where the animals rested in the shade, and a moment later he returned with the cart and the pack donkey. Jesus climbed into the back, where two lambs had been tossed in case they ran out of provisions. Tobias cracked a whip over the mule that drew the cart. As they pulled away, colored banners hung from the trees in anticipation of cheering the messiah on his way to Jerusalem.

The lambs bleated in distress, sensing that they were being torn from home. For some time, Jesus whispered soothingly to them, but he neither looked at nor spoke to Tobias. He didn't want to reveal what it had cost him to make his brutal speech.

That night, exhausted with praying, the Essenes disbanded. Some were so spent that they spread blankets on the floor of the hall to sleep. Most gathered their things and headed back to their isolated homesites in the hills. The mood was forlorn. Night came and went. The next morning, when those who had slept in the hall woke up, they found that the paintings on the walls had disappeared, leaving the plaster as fresh and white as the day it was first applied.

AFTER LEAVING THE Essenes Jesus kept close to the river Jordan, which gave Tobias hope that he would enter Jerusalem after all, or at least turn homeward to Galilee. "Don't you want to see your mother and say farewell?" he asked.

Without turning to look back, Jesus said curtly, "My mother knows where I am."

The worst thing would be if Jesus was headed for the notorious Silk Road that ran from the Nile to the outer darkness in the East. Since boyhood Tobias had heard about fantastic courtesans carried in a litter covered by cloth of gold, princesses turned to whores for the delectation of Roman emperors. Their camels wore silver bells, and the wafting of roses and ambergris could be smelled an hour before they arrived. Mile-long spice trains traveled the route, and the rainbow-hued silk, supposedly spit out by worms, felt like the softest lambskin sliced into layers you could see the moon through. The Silk Road led to oblivion.

But on the third day Tobias recognized the road to Syria instead, one of the most dangerous in Palestine for its smugglers and masked brigands. He had traveled it in his wandering, years ago, when he set out to find Jesus. Every mile had been a terror. Jesus was calm and never asked for news from the traders they encountered. Whenever they came to a crossroads, he silently nodded toward the fork he wanted. Now Damascus was only two days away.

That night at camp Tobias unburdened his heart. "You're leaving our people behind," he said, stirring the ashes dejectedly with a stick.

"That's not the same as leaving God behind," said Jesus. He considered for a moment. "Do you believe there's one God for the Jews and another for everyone else?"

Tobias shook his head. "I know your teaching. There is only one God for all. But haven't the Gentiles rejected him? They have put themselves outside the law. The Jews haven't. That's why we are the chosen people."

Jesus didn't reply. They'd had the same argument many times. Anyway, it wasn't theology that had soured Tobias's mood. The next morning Jesus took the reins from his hands. "You should go back. Unpack the donkey and ride it."

"Alone? It's not safe," Tobias protested.

Jesus seemed determined. "You'll soon run into the caravans heading south. Join them." The unknown places that lay beyond Damascus might as well be mapped in Hell for all that Tobias knew of them.

When he stubbornly climbed into the back of the wagon and hunched down on the straw-covered floor, Jesus said nothing at first.

"You shouldn't have let those two lambs loose," Tobias grumbled. "Somebody or something will eat them. Better it was us."

An hour later they stopped beside a muddy spring to let the mule and donkey drink, and Jesus said, "I can protect your soul. I know it better than you do. But I can't protect your body. You belong among the Jews. Bad as it is with the Romans, the Essenes have found a refuge."

Tobias laughed with more than a trace of bitterness. "So you advise me to save my body and lose my soul? Is that your final teaching?"

This was Tobias's backhanded way of refusing to leave Jesus. It was also the last thing he said before the robbers struck. There were six of them—probably a clan of impoverished Syrians who preyed on travelers as their only way to make a living—hiding in the thick brush watered by the muddy spring. They jumped out with fierce shrieks, brandishing long knives with rippled blades. Tobias had only one chance to save himself. He rose to his feet, shouting and waving his hands.

"Stop, stop!"

He reached into his sash to find the small money bag concealed in it, but the bandits mistook what he was doing.

They thought he was reaching for a dagger. The youngest, an expert thrower, hurled a short spear crudely tipped with hammered iron. Tobias's eyebrows flew up in surprise as the point pierced his throat. He gave one blood-muffled gargle and fell to the ground.

Tobias remained motionless, his eyes raised to the sky.

The Syrians shouted to each other in the local dialect. One knelt over Tobias's body and extracted the money purse. He looked mildly chagrined when he didn't find a weapon, but the tallest bandit, apparently his older brother, kicked at the corpse to show his disdain for remorse. He pressed his face close to Jesus's and screamed something unintelligible. When Jesus didn't answer, keeping his eyes fixed upward, the bandits laughed in derision.

The older one, who had kicked Tobias, reached for Jesus's sash to rip it away, hoping to find more money.

Jesus leveled his eyes at him. "No," he said softly.

The bandit looked quizzically at his arm, which began to tremble visibly. It wasn't paralyzed, but something else must have happened that only the bandit detected. He jumped back with a muttered oath. The other bandits grew quiet. After a pause, the older one turned on them and shouted angrily. An argument ensued, with much pointing at Jesus and waving of knives in his direction. Clearly the other bandits wanted to rob and kill him, and they were confounded that their leader, usually the most vicious one, refused to let them.

Jesus paid no attention. He knelt over Tobias and spoke to him. "Be glad this happened quickly. You would have been furious to think that no one will say Kaddish over you."

The place was too remote and desolate for any proper rituals; there wasn't even a tool to dig a grave with. Jesus took off his white cloak and covered Tobias's body, shielding it from the sun. But he didn't begin the prayers of lamentation demanded in the ritual of Kaddish.

"I release you from your earthly bonds," he whispered. "Go to my Father with joy."

Jesus didn't look over his shoulder. From the silence behind him, he knew that the bandits had left, using their furtive skills to make no sound. Whether they ran away or took up their old hiding places again didn't matter. Jesus held up his hand in blessing over the covered corpse. With the soul gone, it was merely a husk. He glanced at the wagon and the mule and donkey, both skittish from the eruption of violence and the smell of blood in the air. They lingered by the water hole, flicking their ears to sense if more danger was coming.

Jesus walked over and undid their harnesses. He took the pack off the donkey's back and laid it on the ground. From this point on he would walk. He sat for a moment under a palm tree, drinking from the goatskin water bag that he and Tobias carried with them. At one point he smiled to himself. The mystery was leading him onward, and it seemed to operate purely on whim. You would think that the messiah knew the road ahead, but in fact his mind was completely blank. It was as if God wanted him to walk a path where there was no path.

When the sun was no longer at its burning zenith, Jesus swung the water bag over his shoulder and got up. He gave a farewell nod to Tobias and walked away. Another person might have been curious about the blood oozing through the white robe that covered the body. And not from morbid curiosity. It needed explaining why a man pierced through the throat should now be bleeding, hours after his death, from the palms of his hands, his forehead, and a deep gash on his right side. Jesus walked away without asking.

THE ENDLESS ROAD east flowed like a dry river filled with humanity. No one on it could figure out who Jesus was. He had no goods or camels, so he wasn't a merchant. He packed no tent like the nomads and didn't stop by the side of the road to pray like the monks. He carried no sacred relics like the pilgrims. Besides, pilgrims had a destination in mind. Jesus fell in with one, a Persian heading west who had to make a diversion away from the trunk road.

"What do you seek, brother?" the Persian asked.

"Myself," said Jesus.

The Persian laughed. "How do you know you didn't leave that at home?"

"I don't."

They were walking through unusually beautiful terrain, a rippling green steppe that had broken out in glowing yellow wildflowers like sunlight fallen to earth. The Persian was also a trader in stones. "For building?" Jesus asked. "No," the Persian told him. He unfolded a square of raw silk, showing Jesus the most brilliant lapis lazuli he had ever seen, more intensely blue than the Tyrian sea. There was only one place in the known world where such stones came from. The Persian pointed southeast, indicating a place very far away. His family had trekked back and forth for ten generations along the great route east and west, enriching themselves with nothing more than a handful of blue stones.

"I'm rich. I don't need to trade anymore," the Persian said, "but I've heard about the Great Mother in Ephesus who has a thousand breasts. I want to kneel before her."

"Why?" asked Jesus.

"Because I don't want to die before finding God."

"How do you know you didn't leave him at home?"

The Persian was amused and intrigued; he dismounted from his horse and walked beside Jesus for the rest of that day. His best guess was that this lone traveler must be a Jew, but Jesus didn't say yes or no.

"If you won't tell me that, at least tell me why you left," the Persian insisted.

"It's hard to explain. I am not walking away from anything; I am not walking toward anything. If God is everywhere, he cannot be lost nor can he be found. And yet I must travel."

The Persian, who was far from stupid, said, "Either you have looked into this very deeply or you are a simpleton."

Jesus smiled. "A simpleton would have wanted to play with one of your pretty blue stones. Where I come from, no one can figure me out. I've been worshiped; I've been despised."

Without warning Jesus veered off the road, heading for a particularly brilliant patch of wildflowers. The Persian trader stopped, considering what to do. It was worth a few hours talk to while away the boredom of his journey (he knew from experience that this segment of the road, which lasted three months time, was only a fraction of the whole, which went to the end of the world), but it wasn't worth being sucked into the delusions of a madman. Nonetheless, he waited.

After half an hour Jesus returned and resumed walking as if he hadn't detoured at all. The Persian said, "I know where you need to go." He enjoyed the surprised look on Jesus's face. "It will take several months," the Persian continued, "but when you reach the land of horses, where they roam free by the thousands, turn south. The world is a hunchback, and you will reach its hump by heading south. Start climbing. That's what you need to do."

"How do you know?" asked Jesus.

The Persian held up his hands. "It's not what you think. I'm no oracle. But you resemble others I've met. They are called the 'God-mad,' and they come from those mountains. You must climb so high that you can't breathe anymore. The snow will blind you until you think death is just another name for whiteness that never ends. Ordinary people go insane if they stay there too long, but a few become God-mad, which is a different thing." He shrugged his shoulders. "If you believe them."

An hour later the road forked, and the Persian took the side that led to the lapis mines. Jesus kept to the main route. Truth to tell, the stranger had bestowed a valuable clue. Jesus could be God-mad, if that meant consumed by the divine until all else was burned away.

For months an invisible hand had provided for Jesus's needs. When he was hungry, food appeared. Usually this happened as if by chance—he would come across an abandoned camp where a loaf of bread had been inadvertently left behind, or a wild animal might drop part of a lamb it had killed in a ditch. Jesus ate the bread and roasted the lamb, thanking God as he did.

But God had stopped guiding him. Jesus no longer heard any words in his head, much less directions about where he should go. He sat in a glade of dark, fragrant cedars contemplating this change. He didn't feel abandoned or alone. Was God asking for something Jesus hadn't seen? No answer came, and so Jesus concluded that he must be following a mystery so deep that it had no voice. Something so inexpressible that even the burning bush that appeared to Moses would be too crude and gross. Still, he was grateful to get directions from the Persian. Perhaps it was time to hear God's voice in every voice. Or was that the maddest of all?

In a few days Jesus began to follow the nomads through the endless grasslands. In their hide-covered wagons, they were sailors on these green waves where shaggy wild ponies ran by the thousands. These nomads came from the east. Jesus never learned more than a few words of their nasal, sing-song tongue. They gestured for him to jump in the back of their wagon, where silent women and children nestled with the chickens and sheep. He gazed curiously at the women's round faces smeared with lanolin to make them shine. A mark of beauty, he supposed.

Only after several weeks did the roaming band encounter a village. When they did, the men suddenly became ferocious. They lit torches and ran shrieking toward the village. At first sight of them, the villagers ran without a fight. The nomad men looted everything they could lay their hands on—candles, jewelry, tallow, hides. The livestock they killed and butchered on the premises. With equal indifference they slaughtered any man or boy they found cowering in the surrounding grass.

Jesus was shocked. He said a silent blessing over the dead, whom the nomads stripped of ornaments and useful things like leather britches. They had no reason to bury the corpses; these were left among the intestines and other useless parts of the slaughtered stock. Jesus watched as some men approached the wagon he was riding in. They hitched a weaned lamb and two calves to it, animals they could fatten along the way and butcher later. None of the men gave Jesus a second glance.

He wasn't afraid of them, despite their bloody hands, which had been wiped across their faces during the sweaty work of the day, leaving tracks of gore across mouths and foreheads. Only, why hadn't they killed him? The caravan started rolling. In the back of the wagon women crouching on straw mats as they picked through the pillaged spoils stared impassively at Jesus.

Then he understood. There was a circle of peace around him. He had nothing to lose anymore, which made him invisible. He was the wind inside the wind. How strange that God had worked such a change, invisibly and silently. If he wanted, Jesus knew he could wander the face of the earth in perpetual blessing.

Yet he couldn't. To be blessed in a cursed world would become unbearable. He knew that deep inside, and when the grasslands finally came to an end, Jesus left the caravan, taking a fine black horse that the nomads had presented to him, a parting gift. As the Persian had directed, Jesus turned south and came to the hump of the world. He began to climb, and when he reached the bleak terrain where vegetation shriveled to grass half an inch high, God quit providing food. Jesus kept on. Above the snow line even shriveled grass disappeared, and he plunged into the merciless whiteness that the Persian had predicted. The only sign from God to continue was that Jesus didn't freeze to death, despite the bone-chilling cold.

Finally, after another week of riding and walking, Jesus was stopped by an invisible fist in the form of a massive blizzard that descended at twilight. Jesus had been in the mountains for days, and if he wasn't insane or starved, he wasn't God-mad, either. The snow began to pile up in drifts, which built into dunes of snow blown by the howling wind. Jesus had no fire; there was no moon in the sky.

He released his horse, slapping its flanks until the animal trotted away, perhaps to survive on its own. The blinding whiteness of snow in the daytime turned suffocating and black at night. As the drifts mounted up to his chest, Jesus flailed his arms like a swimmer caught in heavy surf.

Soon this proved too exhausting. With no chance of escape, Jesus knelt and began to pray. By tucking his chin into his chest he kept the snowflakes from filling his nostrils.

Minutes turned into hours, or so it seemed. Eventually the weight of the snowpack buried him.

Which is how I found him, thanks to the temple lad who sighted an unusual hump in the snow the next morning.

14

THE WAGER

The story I've unfolded took four days for Jesus to relate. By that time he had learned to brew tea almost as well as I could. (He was considerate and brewed it weak after the second day.) In fact, he learned to do everything. There was little to it. Each meal was the same and entailed the same ritual. Pile chips of dried dung to build a fire in the stone hearth. Boil a pot of water from snow gathered at the doorstep. Once the water was hot, throw in strips of dried meat from the supply that hung from the rafters. Add a handful of millet (first picking out the weevils) and let the pot boil until the whole formed a sticky mass.

If measured by pots of sticky millet and jerky, Jesus's life story had taken twenty-three. I had listened without visible reaction while he talked; my eyes closed, but I never fell asleep.

We ate the twenty-third pot, and he stood up to fetch the tea, saying, "Has this taught you anything about me?"

I shrugged. "I knew all I needed to know before you began to talk. Has the journey taught *you* anything? That's the question."

Jesus smiled. "I learned strange things. At first I was a seeker, but whatever I found turned to dust in my mouth. Then God performed miracles through me, but I had nothing to do with them."

"And now?"

"Now I've vanished. I can barely find myself."

"Is that so bad?" I asked.

Jesus hesitated. "May I speak the truth? I thought God would exalt me."

His look would have made some people laugh and others pity him. I said, "Exaltation comes when there's nothing left of you for the world to grab. Be patient. God has already erased you. I see barely a smudge."

I fiddled with a string of beads dangling from my neck, not looking up to see if Jesus was surprised. "The minute I set eyes on you, I thought of an animal common in these mountains, the snowshoe rabbit."

Jesus laughed. "I've never seen one."

"The snowshoe rabbit is brown in the summer when the snow has melted. It blends into the rocks and dirt so the foxes can hardly see it. Then it turns white in the winter when the blizzards come. But there's a fox that can turn just as white, so the rabbit is still in danger, and the struggle continues."

Jesus set the small iron teapot down between us. "I don't understand."

"You will."

Suddenly I began swatting at the air like someone shooing away summer flies. Jesus asked what I was doing.

"Keeping the demons away," I replied. "Use your eyes."

Jesus couldn't see what I was talking about at first. But if he squinted hard, he detected something on the edge of visibility: flitting shadows in the sunbeams that streamed in through the cracked window. "Do they torment you?" he asked.

"Just the opposite. They love me; they can't stay away. Shoo!"

I tilted my head quizzically. "And you? Has God given you the gift of demons?"

"I never thought they were a gift. Do you know who Job is?" Jesus asked. I shook my head. "In the scriptures of my people," said Jesus, "God and the Devil made a wager. They found one man named Job who believed in God with his whole heart. He lived in complete righteousness in the land of Uz. The Devil wagered with God that he could turn anyone against God, even Job."

"Ah," I murmured. "And you consider this God benevolent? I won't ask who won."

"Because you already know?" said Jesus.

"No, because the wager is still on. Only this time they're betting over you."

Jesus regarded me sipping my tea. He had followed a mystery to the end, and the end was a miserable hut in a desolate rock field engulfed in snow. Who was I, anyway? It was easy enough to read his doubts.

I said, "It doesn't matter who I am. You want God to win the wager, don't you?"

"Yes."

"Well, the odds are against him. In fact, the odds are zero. More tea?"

Jesus shook his head. "Why are they zero? Are the Jews cursed forever?" He thought about the mark of Cain and tried to put the image out of his mind.

"This Devil you speak of, what's his name?"

"Satan. We know him as the Adversary."

I gave a sharp nod. "That says it all. You want human suffering to end. You want a world based on purity and virtue. God has heard your prayers. He gave you miracles; he imparted strength and truth. So what's stopping you? Not a curse. You ran into your adversary, someone who will keep pushing human beings in the opposite direction no matter how hard you push them toward God."

I paused, giving the air a vigorous swipe; the swarm of flying imps was coming too close. "They know I'm talking about them," I explained. "Demons are eternal. This Satan won't ever go away, and as long as he persists, the chances of God winning the wager are zero."

"Why?"

"Because humans aren't eternal. He has time to pick them off one by one."

Jesus lowered his head. This old man had articulated what he most feared. "I had two people close to me, a man who was fierce to save the Jews and a woman who wanted to surrender herself in love for me. Was that Satan's work?"

"Who else?" I said. "The man was jealous of you, the woman wanted to possess you. Demons have a way of blinding people to the light, even when it stands right in front of them."

"She was closest to me," Jesus murmured. "In her I saw mother and wife at the same time. I saw all women. How can that be wrong?"

"Then find a way to marry all women," I said. "On your path that will be possible. When one woman's love is the same as God's love, you will know women as divine."

I leaped to my feet. "Let's see if we can track down one of those rabbits I told you about," I said.

This baffled Jesus, but he raised no argument—he knew it was his role to submit to the mystery brought his way. For the moment I embodied the mystery and spoke with its voice.

We wrapped ourselves in animal skins and stepped out into a bitter cold. The day was clear as crystal, which made the snow glare painfully. Jesus looked down, his hand over his eyes, and followed my footprints as I led the way. We tramped through the new snow left by the blizzard until I suddenly stopped, holding a finger to my lips. "Ssh."

I froze in place for a long minute, then crept forward, trying not to make crunching noises as my soles punched through the snow crust.

"There," I said, pointing. "We've gotten very close to one, a big male. Do you see him?"

Jesus looked where I indicated, but the snowfields were so white that his eyes rebelled and began to swim with blue—their retinas were overloaded.

"I can't see anything," he said.

"Are you sure?"

Jesus strained, but the light's intensity made it too painful to gaze for more than a few seconds. It amazed him that I could keep staring.

"All right," I said. "Close your eyes. Let them rest. I don't want to have to lead you home by the hand."

Jesus crouched with his eyes shut, his hands over them. Gradually the blue glare faded away. He could feel me crouching beside him.

"This has been an excellent lesson," I said with satisfaction.

"A lesson about what?"

"About you. You couldn't see the rabbit because it was white on white. People can't see you because you are God on God. The whole world shines with divine light, yet it so blinds everyone that they can't spot God when he shows up in person."

Jesus took his hand away from his eyes. "Don't say that. No man can be God. Among my people saying that's a sacrilege."

The rebuke didn't bother me; it made me laugh. "What are you saying? That God must bow to the rules of people who can't even see him?"

"I thought you said they were blinded by seeing him everywhere." Jesus felt the onset of a stabbing headache; he had taken his hand away from his eyes too soon.

I said, "I spoke the truth. People don't know that they see God everywhere. They think they see trees and hills and clouds. That's what blindness does. It hides reality behind a veil." I got to my feet. "You scared the rabbit away. Let's go home."

Jesus didn't protest. It would be a relief to get back to the hut; a place that was warm and dim might make his headache go away. But as we tramped back, his mind kept protesting about something.

He said, "You mustn't call me God anymore."

"All right. Soon I won't have to."

"Why is that?"

I turned to face him, my breath clouding in the frigid air and crystallizing as frost on my cheeks. "You're out to be greater than God. Admit it. There's no use hiding."

"What?" Jesus was genuinely shocked. "I'll listen to your lessons and try to figure out your riddles, but not if they're insane."

I ignored the objection. "You want to change the world. You said so yourself. God was content merely to create it.

He doesn't interfere. So if you want to be the great meddler, you must want to be greater than God."

Jesus looked baffled. My logic made sense, and I certainly seemed satisfied with it. I hummed to myself the rest of the way back to the hut. Jesus had no choice but to follow. The blizzard had covered over any trace of a trail going downslope, and anyway, if he left now, he risked two things: never discovering how I made demons love me, and certain death from wandering aimlessly in the whiteness where the God-mad are born.

THAT NIGHT JESUS ate his bowl of sticky millet in silence. I, who love solitude much better than company, watched him without saying a word. I also knew that Jesus's mind was worrying over the things that had been said. The hut was so cramped that the two of us had to sleep on the floor side by side, our shoulders almost touching. We lay on our backs staring at the ceiling, each aware that the other was awake.

Sometime well after midnight Jesus said, "Why did you come up here to live?"

"I had to. The alternative was suicide." I was full of surprises, and I dropped this one matter-of-factly. "I even brought a knife in case I'd have to do the deed. It's over there." I indicated a cabinet in the corner. Jesus couldn't see the gesture, because the room was pitch-black.

"Why suicide?" he asked.

"Because I was like Job and like you. I looked around, and the whole world seemed to be fighting a war between God and the demons. People staggered blindly between pleasure and pain. They cried out for God when God was everywhere. What's the use of living in such a world if you can't change it?"

"But you didn't kill yourself."

I chuckled in the dark. "No. That foolishness went away the first week. Being so damn cold, I thought killing myself would be a favor, and I was too miserable to do anyone a favor."

Jesus turned his head in my direction. "Am I as strange as you?"

"You can't guess?"

We both laughed. Then Jesus said, "So if you didn't kill yourself, you must have changed the world."

"Oh yes."

"How?"

"The same way you're going to. And it won't take long to show you. How many years did you live with the Essenes, five? You'll be able to change the world in five seconds, once you know the truth."

"Which is what?"

"The truth I am about to tell you," I said, "would mean nothing to an ordinary man. You don't realize it, but you are the rarest of the rare. You were born only to serve God, and yet that's not what makes you rare. Others have been born, many others, who only wanted to serve God. You, however, are like a feather poised on the edge. You don't need a shove. I can tip you over with a breath."

Jesus lay there on the hard floor, wrapped in thick goatskin, but still colder than he ever imagined he would be. The darkness was as profound as the darkness in a cave. His senses detected nothing except the low voice of an old man speaking close to his ear. Could this really be the setting for a revelation? He waited.

Before I could utter another word, the door flew open with a bang. Startled, Jesus half sat up. The moon was bright over the snowfields. In its eerie light a figure was outlined in the doorway.

"Don't be startled," I said. I was relaxed and confident. "It's to be expected."

"Who is it?" Jesus whispered. The figure didn't move or speak. It looked vaguely human, but there was little doubt that it wasn't.

"Your adversary is worried," I said. "He wants to stop me."

For an instant Jesus saw an image in his mind of a white rabbit pounced on by a white fox, the rabbit squirming helplessly in the fox's jaws until its neck cracked and it went limp. The next instant the doorway was empty, and the shadowy figure was in the room. A cloud passed over the moon. Now the only way to detect the intruder's presence was by the faint padding of his footsteps on the floor.

Should I be afraid? Jesus wondered.

I answered. "Not if you are who I think you are." I raised my voice. "You should listen too. You'll learn something."

In response there was a harsh growl close to where we lay; the room was filled with a fetid odor. A wave of cold terror struck Jesus in the chest.

His body trembled, but he felt my hand on his shoulder. "Steady. Ignore him, and listen. You already know that God is everywhere. But you haven't taken the next step, which is why you wandered the face of the earth until you found me. I am here to give you the knowledge that will provide the final release. If God is everywhere, he is in you. If he is in you, then you are everywhere. Do you understand?"

Jesus trembled as if struck by a terrible fit; my words had struck deep. He no longer heard me speaking. But someone did. The voice of God had been absent for many months. Now it returned again, only this time it was also Jesus's voice, the two so blended that they couldn't be told apart.

"You cannot change the world as long as you are a person. As one man, you will never escape the war between good and evil."

At this the intruder growled menacingly, and Jesus saw two eyes glowing red in the dark. But the threat was useless. The voice continued.

"Only someone who knows the reality beyond good and evil can know me. I am in all things, without division. This Satan wants you to believe that he rules a place where I am not. But even he is made of God."

The glowing red eyes darted closer, and when they were directly over Jesus, they shot fire. The voice went on, "The Adversary doesn't want anyone to know this, because it would destroy his power. He can hardly admit it to himself. If he is God, the war between us comes to an end, and he thrives on war."

Suddenly the intruder emitted a deafening shriek. The walls of the hut shook. Tears rolled down Jesus's cheeks. I whispered close his ear. "The final stroke must come from you. It can never be taught, only discovered within. Keep listening."

Jesus regained control with difficulty. The voice waited and then it said, "Only someone who can see the demons as part of God is free. Good and evil dissolve. The veil drops away, and all you see is divine light—inside, outside, everywhere. The sight of a rotting corpse becomes as blessed as a rainbow. There is no reality but the light, and you are that light. Your soul is the world's soul. In your resurrection will be the resurrection of the world."

The whole time it spoke, Jesus held his breath without knowing it. Now he released it in one long sigh. Mysteriously, as the air left his lungs it was replaced by a warm glow. The sensation was strange. His whole body seemed to deflate, but when he looked inside, Jesus saw what was really happening. Every experience he had ever had was leaving him. He saw a swarm of memories flowing out, like countless fluttering birds flying out of a tree at dawn.

I whispered again. "Let them all go. Lose yourself. It's the only way you will ever find yourself."

This opened the floodgates inside. Jesus saw the glowing red eyes move toward the door. Without knowing why, he sprang up to follow. I didn't stop him. The eyes drifted away from the hut. Were they really Satan's or merely some phantom's? The next thing Jesus felt was a blast of frigid air over his naked body. He was running barefoot over the crusted snow, his heels punching deep as he ran. The snowfield was so white that it made the moonlight seem to come from below as much as above.

Let me see you.

Jesus willed his thought to catch up to the Adversary. The glowing eyes turned on him, and a shadowy body began to take shape. Jesus kept running, holding out his arms to embrace it. But the apparition disappeared, and his arms circled around smoke. Jesus bent over panting with exhaustion and stitches of pain in his ribs. The eeriness of the moonlight made him feel as if he were floating in midair. Only the icy cold beneath his feet told him he was still on earth.

FOR SEVERAL DAYS Jesus lay in a state as still as death, but sweating with fever. When he opened his eyes again, he felt weak and drained.

"You inhaled the demon's smoke," I said calmly. "He couldn't hurt you, but he could leave his stink." I put a compress of herbs and packed snow against his forehead.

Jesus sat up weakly. "He doesn't seem to love me the way your demons love you."

"Not yet. Satan has more to lose than a small demon does. For a while he'll avoid you. But eventually you'll meet again."

Once the fever was completely gone, Jesus had a hard time telling that anything had really changed. In fact, he felt hollow, as if God had left him, once again, to his own devices.

I went about my daily routine, and Jesus tried to join in. His heart was no longer in it, though; he felt restless. Remarkable things had happened in the small hut, he was sure of that. Why, then, did he feel bored and ready to leave?

"Once you solve the mystery, it's all a bit flat," I said. "I know the feeling."

Jesus asked me to explain. We were sitting on the doorstep, feeling the feeble heat of the sun. Spring wasn't far away. The vast snowfields were the same dazzling white, but a steady drip from the icicles hanging on the eaves told of new warmth.

"To know God, you must become God," I explained. "People don't want to hear that. It upsets their fantasy that

God sits far away above the clouds. But being God doesn't mean that you created the universe. God did that. He fashioned time out of eternity. He made the heavens and the earth from wisps of his mind. When I say that you've become God, I mean that you know what you're made of." I smiled. "Luckily, I found out before I turned into this withered old stick."

It was the last talk we had on the subject, or almost the last. A few days later I packed some dried meat and millet into a leather bag.

"Here," I said when Jesus came in from washing himself in the snow. He nodded. There were no other preparations to make. Jesus could leave anytime he wanted, but I suggested that we share one last pot of twig tea.

I waved my hands over the teapot. This time I wasn't shooing away demons. "See this steam?" I said. "It doesn't look like the water in the pot, and nothing like the snow I gathered to melt. Nor does it look like a river or rainfall or the sea. But appearances are deceiving: Steam, ice, and water are all the same thing. To know that is to be free of ignorance."

Jesus understood, but he was troubled. "I still feel like myself. Why?"

I shrugged. "Who ever said that being God is a thrill?"

Jesus smiled. "Be serious."

"Who said God is serious? There's a universe to watch over. He has to laugh just to put up with us."

But I knew he craved an answer. I said, "Any piece of knowledge is limited. A fact, no matter how true, barely chips away at the vast field of ignorance. You came to me wanting to know the whole truth. And now you do, but your knowledge is young. Let it ripen. And no matter what happens, either everything is a miracle or nothing is."

At that moment the temple lad reappeared. The latest blizzard had half buried the village, he explained. He hadn't been able to make it through until now. "The priest and I prayed for you," he said, grateful that I was still alive. Even for that bleak region, the cold had been fierce.

"Why pray?" I smiled. "Were you afraid for my soul? I told you I forgot to bring one. It was too heavy to carry, and I needed the room in my knapsack."

The boy didn't like being teased. "If you died, I wanted you to go to Heaven. If you were alive, a few extra prayers couldn't hurt. That's what the priest said."

I thanked him and pressed a small coin into his hand to cover the cost of incense. Then I told the temple lad to escort the stranger to the village and as far down the valley as it took to get to where the snow was gone and the trail became clear.

Without ceremony Jesus left. The temple lad had been confined indoors for days; now he couldn't help running ahead on the trail, which was no more than a rut in the snow. Jesus didn't bid farewell or look back at my hut. There was no chance that I would be standing on the threshold watching.

Jesus didn't suppose that the boy noticed, but when they were within sight of the village, he asked Jesus why he didn't tell the old man good-bye.

"I only say good-bye when I'm leaving," said Jesus. "But I have no place to leave from and no place to go. I used to. Not anymore."

The boy shrugged; he assumed that the stranger talked this way because of the thin air. Or maybe he had become

God-mad. The priest had informed the boy that this phenomenon existed.

A few hours later they reached a cleft between the rocks that acted as a sun trap. The snow was melted there, exposing the trail cut out of the mountainside. The temple lad pointed. "Just go downhill. You won't get lost."

Jesus nodded and thanked him. As he set off on his own, the boy watched him for a few minutes before the trail dipped out of sight. The stranger hadn't talked much on the way down. The temple lad asked his name, but the answer was nonsense. Alpha and Omega weren't proper names, and anyway, they were two names, not one.

15

LIGHT OF THE WORLD

After Jesus left my hut, there was nothing else I could do but watch from afar. Many versions exist of what became of him. I'll tell you what I saw.

A small party on horseback followed the Jordan as it wound like a speckled serpent through the desert. The two riders were making their way north from Jerusalem to Tiberias, the gaudy capital where Herod lived in powerless decadence. He wasn't so much a king as a royal puppet.

"Look, down there. What's going on?" the Roman said. He was a veteran horse soldier named Linus. He claimed to be descended from a line of senators, but in fact he was born in the gutters of Ostia, where the Tiber flows into the sea, carrying the port's sewage with it.

The Jew, who had been lagging in the heat of the day, caught up.

"Where?" he asked.

Linus pointed upstream to a crossing formed by a low spot in the streaked brown rock formations that lined the Jordan, a convenient place to ford cattle across.

Linus, who was lean and battle-hardened, scowled. "Is that trouble?" he asked.

His right hand, always ready for a fight, wore a leather gauntlet stitched with iron studs. Now the hand pointed at a group of local villagers who had gathered at the ford, but they weren't crossing, and they had no grazing stock with them.

"It's not rebels. Not out here in the open," the Jew replied. "Besides, half of them are women and children."

The Jew, who happened to be Judas, smiled secretly to himself. Linus hated the fact that some worthless peasants were sleeping in his favorite willow grove. There were other groves along the river, but this one was where he liked to steal from Herod.

Once a month Linus and Judas were sent to carry treasure to Tiberias as Herod's monthly tribute. Most of it came from money changers in the Temple, and Caiaphas ordered Judas to keep the treasure safe. But the Romans, ever suspicious, insisted on sending one of their own along as extra protection.

Judas had made this trip many times, and the ritual was always the same. When the ford came into view, Linus would yawn and announce that he wanted to take a nap in the willow grove. Judas would agree, then keep his eyes closed long enough for the Roman to snatch a handful of silver coins from the saddlebags. Caiaphas shrugged it off as a necessary expense, up to a point.

"Try to get him to split his take with you," he said. "We'll add it to next month's shipment."

But Judas cared little about such things. It had taken him the better part off five years to worm his way into the accounting functions of the Temple. In a perverse way it brought satisfaction that he, a rebel fugitive, should infiltrate so deeply. Most of his compatriots in Simon's band had been killed in reprisal raids. He was certain the Zealots were doomed.

"Let's go," Judas said. "I see frogs crawling in the mud. Don't you Romans believe that frogs come from Hell? Maybe the entrance is nearby."

"Frogs?" said Linus. His eyes narrowed. "Why are you playing me?"

Then he noticed a group of villagers in the water. "Why are they bathing here?" he asked. "I thought you people had places for that."

"The mikvah," Judas mumbled. "I don't know."

Judas knew more than he let on. He'd heard about this new practice of bathing out in the open—baptism. It had begun secretly in caves and cisterns in the hills, but lately had grown more brazen. "They do it for atonement, to wash away their sins," he said.

"Why not simply pay a fine at the Temple like everybody else?" Linus grumbled. He threw up his hands. "Don't explain. Nobody can understand the Jews, least of all a Jew."

"True," said Judas.

He waited for Linus to settle down before saying, "Why don't you ride ahead? My horse is worn out. I'll water him here."

Linus was tempted. He could steal more loot if he were by himself. But he had a hunch that something political was going on. More and more Jews were washing away their sins in preparation for a mythical general who would lead an assault on Jerusalem. But what could one lone soldier (and a

Jew who wasn't as loyal as a barracks cat) do against twenty or thirty peasants, even if they weren't concealing knives in their tunics?

"Are you sure you'll be safe?" he asked.

"A Jew among Jews. I'll be safer than if you came along."

Linus jerked the reins, guiding his horse to make a wide circle around the baptism party. The one in charge, up to his waist in the river, looked like a wild man dressed in raw skins, his beard tangled and matted. He took a young boy by the nape of the neck and plunged his head under water. The boy came up spluttering and smiling.

"Filthy animals," Linus muttered.

Judas was starting to dismount when he noticed that a man who had been sitting under the trees was heading toward him. His hair and beard were still dripping with Jordan water.

How long had it been? Time hardly mattered. Judas would have recognized Jesus in the dark.

"Don't bother getting down," said Jesus. "You ride. I'll walk beside you."

Judas sat back in the saddle. He glanced at the group who had been gathered around Jesus in the shade. They were all on their knees, bowing in his direction.

"I see that things worked out for you," Judas said drily.

"And you escaped from your friends the assassins."

Judas nodded. His black Roman horse headed off at a slow walk, raising lazy puffs of dust under its hoofs. Jesus kept pace with his hand resting lightly on the horse's withers. There was no trace of recrimination in Jesus's eyes. Not that Judas cared—it had been too long.

"Are you the one who baptizes them?"

"No, someone else," replied Jesus. "My cousin. The people consider him holy. Some call him the messiah."

Judas smirked. "A nice family business."

Jesus kept his gaze lowered toward the dust. "We aren't meeting by chance. It was necessary for me to talk to you."

"Why? I'm no threat to you anymore," snapped Judas, surprised at how much anger rose in his voice.

"I offered you salvation once. But you didn't take it." Jesus spoke easily, an old friend picking up a thread of conversation. "I know why you turned away. You were fighting a war inside. You still are."

Judas's body stiffened. "Don't try that. Go back to the fools who believe in you."

"How do you know that isn't you?"

As gently as Jesus spoke, a rush of hostility gripped Judas's chest. It came from a dark lair and penetrated his heart like a talon.

"Your war must end, Judas. There is no more time," said Jesus. "You are being stalked by death. Accept me, and I will save you. But it must be now," he urged.

Judas was speechless. The pain in his chest grew more intense. It could be a spell cast by Jesus to frighten him into submission. Or Linus. He might have slipped him a poisonous tincture so that he wouldn't have to share his spoils anymore. The blood drained from Judas's face; he slumped in the saddle, unable to move.

The next thing Judas knew, Jesus had reached up and touched his breastbone. The talon started to withdraw, and the pain gradually subsided.

"You don't believe me," said Jesus. "Look behind us."

But when he turned around, all Judas saw was a swirling dust devil fifty yards away. It was a common sight in the desert, a small column dirtied with twigs and leaves, but harmless.

"That's nothing," Judas said. He knew that Jesus had powers. Raising the wind could be one of them.

"You don't understand. This is where it becomes unsafe," Jesus warned, keeping his gaze on the swirling plume. The wind picked up suddenly; the dust devil swelled and came closer.

Within seconds the wind became a gale, and Judas's horse grew skittish. The storm was filling the animal's eyes and nostrils with stinging grit. Jesus had to shout to be heard. "Listen to me, Judas. I love you, and you must accept me."

The urgency of the words startled Judas, but an old contempt filled his throat. "Still dealing in mysteries? It's just wind. It will pass."

At that moment they heard a new sound—a horrifying screech coming from inside the dust devil. Panicked, Judas's horse threw him. When he hit the ground, Judas was blinded by dust.

"Damn you!" he shouted. He made a wild swing for his horse's reins, catching empty air instead. The animal had already disappeared into the opaque storm, like a magical horse vanished by a crafty magus.

By this time the dust devil towered thirty feet high. Jesus lifted Judas to his feet.

"Satan has no right to claim you," he shouted in Judas's ear. "Give your soul to God. Accept me."

Even under threat of death Judas was defiant. He opened his mouth to say no when Jesus suddenly stood erect holding his arms out from his sides. Each hand began to glow, at first on a small spot in the center of the palm. It was like a candle shining through an oilskin lamp. All at once the spot turned white, and the next second a beam of light shot out.

Softly Jesus said, "I am the One. God has not forsaken you. Come."

Judas fell with his face in the dust. He had heard the words clearly, despite the howling wind and the dust devil's uncanny screech.

"I accept," he moaned, and blacked out.

Jesus didn't try to revive him. The dust devil had swelled in strength, enough to lift a horse off the ground. Jesus turned and walked directly toward it without so much as swaying. He stepped inside. It grew eerily calm at the center. Jesus looked around. Calmly he raised his hands. The light they emitted wavered and grew weaker.

"Put them out," he called. "I dare you." The light stopped wavering and glowed brighter.

The dust devil howled, and two red eyes appeared in the whirling chaos. Around them formed a dim silhouette that could have been almost human, just as when Jesus and the Adversary first met.

"Come on, do it," Jesus repeated. "Isn't that why you're here, to put out the light of the world?"

But Satan couldn't, any more than he could knock Jesus to the ground. A mocking voice came from the shadowy silhouette. "I bow to you, master. I wish only to please."

"In what way can a demon please me?" Jesus asked.

Look over your shoulder.

Jesus did. Instead of seeing a thick haze of dust, the scene behind him had been transformed. It was as if he'd been lifted in the air on the back of an eagle, and the whole of Palestine was spread out below. He saw the Sea of Galilee sparkling like a blue sapphire in the sun, surrounded by green hills and fields.

It's yours.

Jesus shook his head. "What good to me is trash? I see nothing that's real."

He felt a wave of confusion from the dim, dusty figure.

"Do you still think you're real?" said Jesus. He held up his palms, and their light grew stronger. "What else can you give me?"

"I can show you how to make bread from stones. No one will starve again. You will feed the multitudes."

"What good is life when you steal a person's soul?" said Jesus.

Suddenly the scenery changed. Jesus found himself poised on the highest turret of the Temple in Jerusalem. The view down to the plaza was dizzying. Pilgrims and devotees wandered about like specks; none of them looked up.

I'll throw you down from this height, and you'll die. Is that real enough? Or do you expect God to save you?

"My Father wouldn't waste his time. If you threw me in front of a painting of a pack of lions, would I need saving?"

Jesus held up his hands again, and now the light shot out with so much force that Satan was hurled backward. The eerie quiet inside the storm broke into a deafening din.

"Give up your pride and arrogance," Jesus cried. "Or the light of God will destroy you."

The column of dust writhed furiously, like a serpent caught by the throat. Jesus closed his eyes and began to imagine the world. First he brought the village of Nazareth to mind, and as each house came into view, he filled it with white light from his hands.

"Let this light push away everything unreal," he prayed. "Let Satan's illusions dissolve."

The mud walls and dirt yards of Nazareth started to glow from within. Jesus moved on to the surrounding hills, and as he envisioned their pine trees and olive groves, he filled them with light until they glowed.

What are you doing?

Jesus didn't reply. The process in his mind was speeding up and widening in larger circles. He saw the entire region of Galilee and filled it with light. The old wager over Job's soul was being nullified. Not by anything Jesus said or did. Not by any miracle to dazzle unbelievers. He had gone past all that. The ultimate secret was in his hands.

When a human being is nothing but pure light, unreality is shattered. Jesus was spreading the light everywhere, looking at everything in the world and substituting God for illusion. It took time, but he wanted to be thorough. By the end the Adversary was begging for mercy. The light had squeezed him into the last cramped corner of creation.

The job was finished. It had taken forty days and forty nights. Jesus got to his feet. The Adversary was greatly diminished, but it hadn't given up.

This is only temporary. Men will remember me again.

Jesus shook his head. "The husks of men will remember you. But their souls are safe forever. The wager is won."

Jesus knelt down by Satan's shrunken form. "Don't you wonder why I didn't kill you?" Smiling, he said, "I'm saving you for the day when you love me. It will come."

The dust devil vanished with one last hiss. When Jesus turned around, he saw Judas's motionless body lying on the ground where it had fallen. Despite everything that had happened, Jesus had returned to where he started. For forty days God had kept Judas alive, and when Jesus touched him lightly, Judas sat up. He had no awareness that more than a minute had passed.

"I've made you safe," said Jesus. "You can follow me now."

Judas blinked, looking baffled. "Who are you?" he said groggily.

"I am Jesus, your master."

Judas shakily got to his feet. "Get away. I know no Jesus, and nobody can make me a slave."

If he hadn't been so bewildered, Judas would have struck out at Jesus. His fist was already curled up at his side. His eyes shone with menace.

And then Jesus understood. Satan couldn't harm him, but he could mask the sight of everyone else and blot out their memories. One last trick of the illusionist. Jesus raised his hands to strip the veil away from Judas's mind. Wobbly as he was, Judas put up his fists to ward off an attack.

Jesus hesitated. "It's all right," he said quietly. "If you follow me, it must be because you love me of your own free will."

"Love you? Stranger, you must have lost your mind."

Jesus put his hands down. "Go in peace," he said. "That's all I can do to end your war."

Judas suddenly felt weak and lost. He heard behind him the noise of galloping hooves. Around the bend trotted Linus, leading Judas's horse on a tether.

"Teach a Jew to ride," the Roman said with scorn. "If this horse had gotten away, the stable sergeant would have taken it out of your hide."

Judas nodded. He must have blacked out when his mount threw him. And the stranger who was weak in his wits? Judas turned around, but the road behind him was empty, and the silence of the woods hung in the still, warm air.

JACOB THE WEAVER was one of the best in Magdala, but when an old man marries a young bride, dignity flies out the window. He knew that people laughed at him behind his back. Jacob didn't care. In the autumn of life, God had brought him solace.

"Mary," he called. He didn't have to speak loudly, just enough to be heard over the click-clack of the shuttle running across the loom.

His wife appeared, dusting flour from her hair. Her cheeks were smudged white; it was baking day.

"Can I trouble you, my dear? More indigo. I'm running short."

Mary nodded. "I'll run to the dyer's." Wiping her hands on a rag, she went to fetch her cloak.

Since she had returned to her home village, people found it hard to recognize her. She fell into silent moods, even in the middle of the public market. She covered her face beyond what was required of a married woman, and if a young man looked at her a certain way, Mary shot daggers back at him.

She usually begged off going alone to fetch yarn from the dyer's house, because Elias the dyer was handsome and unmarried. Jacob knew what the problem was. His young wife was more sensitive to gossip than he was.

"It's only natural," he told her, grasping her hands in reassurance. "A lamb is more tender than a tough old ram." Jacob's fingertips were calloused from years of running the shuttle, and Mary shuddered at his touch. But that too was only natural, he thought. Her skin was too soft for his, which was like sandpaper.

Mary left quickly, taking a roundabout route. The dyer's house was only two streets away, but people looked out their windows, and because she had to fetch new yarn twice a week, their mocking eyes burned her as she passed. There was a back way that went through the animal pens that villagers kept behind their houses.

When she got to Elias's back door, her hand hesitated on the latch. In part she paused to inhale the rich scent of the dyes, especially the buttery spice of saffron, from which the dyer extracted a color like spun gold. But there was another reason, and it made her tremble.

Elias felt her presence in the dyeing room before he saw her. Mary came up behind him, very quietly. The air was steamy from the vats of boiled herbs and wildflowers—a village dyer couldn't afford mineral tints like lapis and cobalt. His blue came from indigo, and at that moment Elias was lifting a mass of freshly dyed yarn from the vat. As he swung it toward the drying racks, his torso, stripped naked to the waist, became streaked with purplish blue.

He saw her then. "You. Just a moment."

This was always the instant of humiliation for Mary. Prudery wasn't the cause. She'd been with enough men to erase any traces of that. But Elias made her wait before he embraced her. It wasn't enough that she was betraying her husband; she had to be shown, each and every time, that the dyer was the more desirable one, not her.

Turning around, Mary went alone to the bedroom. She took off her robe and shift and lay down on the low bed. It had a good mattress since the dyer had his choice of wool. He was sensual enough to fill the mattress with the finest lamb's wool. In moments of delight, when Mary was so aroused that she forgot her shame, she loved the soft feeling of it under her back and shoulders.

Elias stood in the doorway wiping his chest to get the stain off. Mary asked him why he was smiling.

"Usually it's the man who's afraid that rouge has gotten on him or the smell of perfume. But with us it's you. How would you explain blue lips to your husband?"

Like many handsome young men, he knew his worth, but Elias wasn't selfish. He showed a real need for Mary, and he took his time loving her. He kissed her breasts, and if he had time he even pulled out a well-worn copy of the Song of Songs and read poetry to her. Some of his tender gestures mattered to her when they happened; none of it mattered afterward.

As chance befell, Elias had missed wiping droplets of dye from his beard, and Mary got up with indigo on the side of her neck where he'd placed his head in the exertions of love. He noticed and wiped the stain away with his wet fingers.

"Look at me," he said, wanting to make sure he'd gotten it all.

"I don't want to."

"Why not?" When Mary didn't answer, pushing herself out of his arms to get dressed, Elias laughed softly. "Strange girl. You didn't have to marry him in the first place. Living with a crab apple doesn't make you lose your taste for ripe cherries."

Suddenly there was a loud rap at the front door. Elias pulled aside the curtains. His face turned grim.

"Who is it?" Mary asked, immediately becoming as anxious as he looked.

"Four men. Run to the back. I'll see you safely out."

The men on the doorstep had seen the curtain part; they knocked more insistently. Elias didn't stop to pull on his clothes. He pulled Mary by the hand to the back door and flung it open. But the town vigilantes weren't acting on the spur of the moment. They had planned in advance, and four more men, scowling and armed with sticks, stood in the back yard by the sheep pen.

Without a word they grabbed Mary and jerked her away from the house.

"No!" Elias shouted.

The four men didn't bother with the naked lover. They dragged Mary away while Elias stood by the door. After a moment he shut it and went back inside.

There was no official wall for stoning criminals as there would have been in Jerusalem. The eight men had a place in mind, however, the side of an abandoned mill. They made a show of marching Mary down the street. She didn't cry or hang her head, even as the townswomen joined the procession, screeching and shouting curses at her. Somebody ran for Jacob, the offended husband, but when he didn't come, the mob grew impatient.

Each man had picked up a stone, and they would have assaulted her then and there. Mary couldn't look at them; she sank down on the ground, numb and shivering.

"What are you doing, brothers?"

Heads turned, and Mary couldn't help but look up. The sight of Jesus brought no flicker of recognition in her.

"We're exacting justice," an elder told the stranger.

"Why?"

"She was found committing adultery. Her sin was still warm on her flesh." The elder eyed Jesus warily. It would be inconvenient if he turned out to be a Roman spy.

"The rabbi gave us permission," someone shouted from the crowd, which was a lie, in hopes of making the stranger think twice.

"But the rabbi isn't here," Jesus pointed out. He kept his gaze on the men and away from Mary. "Why is that?"

When nobody answered, Jesus said, "Could it be because killing is also a sin? I am among Jews, aren't I?"

"Go away. We're in the right," someone else called out.

"If you are, let me find you a bigger stone." Jesus reached down and picked up a jagged rock twice as large as his hand. "As long as one of you is without sin, let him cast the first stone. He has nothing to fear from the Father. Our God only punishes the guilty."

He held the rock up. "Well?"

The men glanced at each other nervously. Jesus dropped the stone from his hand; it clattered loudly on the pile that had been gathered for the execution.

"I will make a bargain with you," Jesus said. He walked over and stooped down, taking Mary by the hand. He lifted her to her feet. "This woman will sin no more. If any of you see even the slightest blemish in her from this day on, I will come and lead the punishment."

Shame had replaced much of the mob's anger, but there were mutters now. "You can't promise such a thing," the elder declared.

"I promise it not only for her, but for all of you. Isn't it written that someone will come to take away your sins? It may be time to believe it."

The mob buzzed. "How can you claim to be the messiah?" the elder said suspiciously.

"What did you expect, a giant who comes down on a chariot of fire?" said Jesus. "So did I, once."

Mary stared at him with the same bewilderment Judas had. She tried to pull away. Jesus whispered in her ear. "You wanted to possess me with your love. Don't you remember?" She began to tremble.

"What are you to this whore?" the elder demanded. "She has a husband. She greatly offended him."

"I am her soul's husband, and I am never offended," said Jesus.

Leading Mary through the crowd, Jesus looked right and left. "I bring good news from God, enough to fill the world. First I must take this woman to be purified."

Mary was in a daze, aware only that they weren't being followed. A few minutes later she passed Jacob the weaver's house, which was shuttered and bolted. Jesus saw her eyeing it.

He said, "Leave that life behind. The Lord has prepared the way before me."

This wasn't enough to calm her heart, and soon they were away from the town. A stream ran by the side of the road; she could wash away the dust and tears from her face.

"And that last smudge of blue," Jesus said, smiling.

Mary flushed with shame, but when she knelt by the water and splashed her face, more than dust and tears came away. Around her reflection shone a brilliance like the sun at noon, and Jesus's hand was poised over her. With a gasp Mary whirled around. For the briefest second Jesus was haloed, and the next second the radiance disappeared.

Awestruck, she could barely whisper, "Who are you?"

"The one the world waits for. But I come to you first."

"Why?

"Because I know what will purify you of sin forever."

You would have expected fresh tears to pour down Mary's cheeks, from relief and gratitude, or if nothing else, the aftershock of fear. But Mary didn't cry. In quiet wonder she said, "What have you done to me?"

"I have given you this day new life," he said gently.

She would see him repeat the same blessing over and over, from that moment until the end came. A terrible end, but Mary had no way to foresee that. It often fell to her to help dazed people to their feet after Jesus held his hand over them.

"What just happened?" they'd mumble, those that could find any words—most couldn't.

"He killed who you were, so that who you are can be born."

It was a good answer even though the disciples who spent hours memorizing what Jesus said overlooked it. But words hardly mattered. Jesus had opened a window on eternity, and Mary gazed out for the rest of her life.

THE NEWS OF the execution took days to reach Nazareth, so the village slept peacefully for a while longer. Passover week brought feasting that lasted half the night. Amazingly, Isaac the blind rose from his sickbed to attend. His youngest daughter, Abra, led him by the hand. He couldn't see the decorations—silk satin, precious hangings and banners stored in cedar chests all year long, or groaning tables piled high with sweetmeats. But Isaac remembered them vividly from years ago.

"All this for the angel of death?" he said.

Abra was embarrassed. "God saved the Jews from the angel of death, and delivered us out of Egypt. You know that," she said, looking the other guests apologetically. "You'll excuse him, he's old."

"Don't forget sick," said Isaac cheerfully. "Old and sick."

Abra celebrated too much at the feast and fell asleep in a chair before dawn. Isaac's other daughters were already at home in bed. He thanked God for providing him the right moment to escape. Using his cane, Isaac crept outside and tapped his way until he reached the edge of town, where the fragrant pinewoods began.

The old man felt less secure here beyond the last house in the village. Which way did the Lord want him to go? A faint breeze blew on his right cheek, a sign to turn left. Isaac thanked God again. He turned his steps, stumbling over stony ground and twice almost fell; he stopped and waited patiently for another word from God. None came, and then with the acuity of the blind he sensed someone close by.

"Jesus?" Isaac mumbled. His latest sickness had made him alarmingly frail and emaciated. He didn't have the strength to go any farther.

Jesus's voice said, "Here I am."

"I dreamed of you last night," said Isaac. He fumbled in the air to find where Jesus was.

"Better not to touch me," Jesus said. "Not just yet."

"Ah." Isaac understood. His dream had showed him everything. The crown, the blood dripping down Jesus's forehead.

The crushing weight on his shoulders as the crowd jeered and mocked. When he woke up that morning, Isaac was trembling. It was all he could do not to betray himself with tears in front of Abra.

But Jesus didn't sound sad, and so Isaac wouldn't be either. "I told you, you have the gift. Maybe more than me. We'll leave that for God to decide," he said.

Isaac felt a puff of warm breath on his cheek. It brought the sweetest feeling, a child's innocence blending with a mother's bliss. Neither one by itself could really describe it.

Isaac couldn't hold back his tears now. They flowed without shame. "Am I dying today also?"

"I don't think that's possible, unless I died. I didn't," said Jesus. "No one ever will again."

Isaac gave a deep sigh. "That's good."

His limbs grew heavy, and he sank to the ground. The rocky ground felt soft as feathers. A new sensation filled his eyes. Was this what they called light? The only light he'd ever known was in dreams. This light was far more vibrant—it quivered with life. Isaac was dazzled by the light of day. He looked up, and Jesus stood over him dressed in a white robe, his expression full of compassion. Isaac couldn't speak.

"God has opened your eyes to see a mystery," Jesus said. "I have walked the earth as the son of man, and he is suffering at this minute. Disciples weep at the foot of the cross. Romans jeer and torture him."

"So I've seen," Isaac said. "It was horrible."

Jesus shook his head. "It was no more than a dream to me. I don't come to you as the son of man, but the Son of God. Therefore, rejoice."

Isaac wanted more than anything to believe Jesus's words.

"You will believe sooner than the rest. Haven't you always said that God is in everything?" said Jesus.

"True. Even if you were a wicked demon sent to taunt me, you must be God."

"I am the messiah, Jacob. The world's long wait is over. And yours."

Suddenly there was no difference between the light of day and the figure of Jesus. His radiance was joyous and unbearable at the same time.

Then Isaac felt Jesus lifting him in his arms like a child. The old man's blindness had returned.

"Will you come with me?" asked Jesus. "I want to meet our Father."

Isaac felt weary to the bone. He couldn't summon the strength to say yes. But he must have, because Jesus's warm breath covered his face like a benediction, and then—silence.

When Abra woke up from her drunken sleep, she felt a guilty pang, followed by a desperate hope that her sisters had taken their father home. But the search party that found his body in the woods was already marching with a shroud-wrapped corpse into Nazareth. Abra could hear women wailing as she stepped outside.

Tears came to Abra's eyes, and she began praying for the departed. But she didn't wail. Isaac was old and infirm. God had showed him mercy. She caught up with the procession and touched the shroud. Its whiteness brought Abra peace. The city of God must be as white as this.

Grief started to rise in her heart, but the peace remained. After all, the messiah would soon appear. Everyone in Nazareth said so, and Abra was the kind to believe.

EPILOGUE

As you know, the local villagers are superstitious about me. Since they consider me a master of black magic and I consider them a nuisance, we keep our distance. In time most of them ceased thinking about me. I became like a twisted tree surviving on the wind-blown summit. Another gnarled pine that kept living out of sheer defiance.

So it amazed the temple lad—now almost old enough to take over from the priest—when I disappeared. The lad trudged up to the hut with an armload of wood one spring morning, only to find the door flung open. It must have been open for a while, judging by the way the wind had scattered my meager possessions and overturned my chair.

Nobody ever saw me again.

Far below, where the mountain people never venture, caravans grew more numerous now that the winter storms were past. I had trekked down and taken a place by the side of the road, watching. One day a wagon stopped, and a traveler dismounted. He walked a few paces and knelt on the ground. In his hands he grasped a small wooden cross.

I waited some minutes before saying, "I knew him."

The traveler's head swiveled around. "How? I'm the first disciple to come this way."

I shrugged. "Even so."

I made a gesture for him to join me—a pot of twig tea was brewing on the brazier. The traveler accepted, out of more than courtesy. He began to talk. He had been a disciple of Jesus almost from the beginning. Eager words tumbled from his mouth about the messiah, about miraculous conversions spreading like wildfire. Many had seen the resurrected Christ, he said. The thrill of his story made the traveler, whose name was Thomas, so excited that he forgot to drink his tea.

When I pointed this out, Thomas smiled secretly. "Man does not live by tea alone."

I asked about Judas.

Thomas was astonished that I, who looked as shriveled as an old monkey, knew Judas's name. He shook his head.

"A traitor and a demon who deserved to hang."

Which Judas had done by his own hand, after throwing Caiaphas's silver back in his face.

"He hanged himself from a tree that was in full bloom," Thomas said, "and overnight the white flowers turned blood red.

I nodded. "So, Judas will be cured and you will be the blessed Thomas. Good." It takes vice to make virtue palatable. Thomas regarded me suspiciously.

"It's the truth," he insisted. "I put my hand is Jesus's wounds after he rose from the dead, and that's true too."

I started smothering the fire in the brazier, which sent up dirty dung-fueled smoke. "Truth is as mysterious as God himself."

The wagon driver was shouting at Thomas now; they had fallen too far behind the rest of the caravan. Reluctantly Thomas got to his feet. He wanted another crack at me.

"Would you follow my master if I proved to you that he rose from the dead?"

"No," I said. "I'll follow him because I have to."

Thomas was baffled. But he waited by the wagon while I gathered my brazier and knapsack. I could have ridden inside, but I insisted on walking behind. I walked through merciless storms, suffered the taunts and rocks of village boys driving Thomas out of town, sucked dirty water from a cloth dipped in mud when a watering hole proved to be dried up.

Where were we going? I didn't ask and didn't care. I owed this to Jesus. I had challenged him to change the world, and he had done it. The light preceded us everywhere. I slept out gazing at the stars. They looked like tiny openings to a world beyond. Sometimes I went to the bright line etched between this world and that. I met Jesus there. We never talked but simply bathed in the radiance that conquers all illusions.

I didn't tell Thomas about these journeys. He would have believed me. But he would never have believed that Jesus brought Judas along.

"You are a great soul," I told Judas. "You were willing to play the villain on earth. You must love Jesus very much."

Judas was modest about accepting praise. All he would say was, "The earth is God's child. How could I not help a child?" It was understood among us that without Judas, there couldn't be this new thing, Christianity.

Of course, it's not such a new thing anymore. A hanging tree is sometimes called the Judas tree. Thomas is the Blessed Thomas. All of which was necessary. For what? For the moment in every soul's life when the veil falls, and beneath all show of rich and poor, sickness and health, life and death, creation sings one word.

Hosanna.

READER'S GUIDE

Jesus and the Path to Enlightenment

The tale is finished, and by the end Jesus has become enlightened. He sees God as pure light infusing every corner of creation. Just as the New Testament Jesus calls his disciples, including Judas, "the light of the world," the Jesus in this novel sees God even in the man who will betray him. Nothing can be excluded from God, including evil itself, in the form of Satan.

Is this how Jesus actually felt? Is this how he became the messiah? Many readers will say no, and with good reason. As believing Christians (or not) they conceive of Jesus as static. He didn't have problems, and he didn't evolve. Jesus was born divine in a stable in Bethlehem and remained that way for the rest of his life.

A static Jesus stands outside human experience, and if that makes him unique—the one and only Son of God—it also creates a gap. For two thousand years this gap has been uncrossable. Millions of people have worshiped Christ without being transformed. With the exception of a handful of saints, Christianity has not turned believers into the "light of the world," even though Jesus clearly intended for that to happen, just as he intended the Kingdom of God to descend to earth in his lifetime. Like Buddha and every other enlightened person, Jesus wanted his followers to become enlightened too.

Indeed, the only way to follow Christ's teachings is to reach his own state of consciousness. To achieve Christ-consciousness, in my view, means walking the path to enlightenment that he walked. For that reason, the Jesus of this novel faces everyday doubts and contradictions. He wonders why God allows evil to triumph so often. He feels inadequate to change other people. He is torn between love for men and women and divine love. In other words, Jesus sets out to solve the deepest mysteries of life—this is the chief reason he isn't static, as the biblical version of Jesus often seems to be.

An impossible teaching?

I fully understand that confirmed Christians take church teachings quite seriously; disturbing their image of Jesus is upsetting. But the Jesus found in the New Testament already raises huge contradictions. Try and put yourself in the place of a first-century person—not necessarily a Jew—who has never heard of Jesus until one day you pass by a large crowd gathered on a hillside to hear this wandering preacher. Out of curiosity you listen too.

> Blessed are the poor in spirit, for theirs is the kingdom of heaven.
> Blessed are those who mourn, for they will be comforted.
> Blessed are the meek, for they will inherit the earth.
>
> MATTHEW 5:3–5

Stop there. Try as hard as we might, it's all but impossible to hear the Sermon on the Mount with innocence. Every word has been totally absorbed into Western culture, has been held up too long as both a promise and an ideal.

> Blessed are the pure in heart, for they will see God.
> Blessed are the peacemakers, for they will be called children of God.
> Blessed are those who are persecuted for righteousness' sake, for theirs is the kingdom of heaven.
>
> MATTHEW 5:8–10

Beautiful as these words are, consider how easy it remains to dismiss them. The poor in spirit don't seem blessed; they are mostly ignored, if not cursed. Millions who mourn aren't comforted. The earth seems to have been inherited by the wealthiest and most ruthless.

There's something disturbing about a gospel that never came true. Or if that sounds too harsh, a gospel that demands more of human nature than we are willing to give. The Sermon on the Mount continues with many unworkable teachings. For example, "You have heard that it was said, 'An eye for an eye and a tooth for a tooth.' But I say to you, Do not resist an evildoer" (Matthew 5:38–39).

Is such a commandment remotely possible to follow? What about the urge to combat evil on behalf of good? Everything from crime control to "good wars" is based on the premise that evil must be resisted. Jesus's famous phrase about turning the other cheek comes next in the sermon, leading to even greater improbabilities: "But if anyone strikes you on the right cheek, turn the other also; and if anyone wants to sue you and take your coat, give your cloak as well; and if anyone forces you to go one mile, go also the second mile. Give to everyone who begs from you, and do not refuse anyone who wants to borrow from you" (Matthew 5:39–42).

As advice for material existence, the sermon is utterly baffling. Jesus tells his listeners not to plan for the future or to save money: "Do not store up for yourselves treasures on earth, where moth and rust consume and where thieves break in and steal; but store up for yourselves treasures in heaven" (Matthew 6:19–20). Taken literally, Christ even asks his followers not to earn a living: "Therefore I tell you, do not worry about your life, what you will eat or what you will drink, or about your body, what you will wear. Is not life more than food, and the body more than clothing? Look at the birds of the air; they neither sow nor reap nor gather into barns, and yet your heavenly Father feeds them. Are you not of more value than they?" (Matthew 6:25–26).

The sermon's whole tendency is to contradict our instincts about how to live in the world. Why did Jesus want us to go against human nature? I don't think he did. He wanted us, instead, to be transformed, which means going beyond the lower self with its ego-driven urges. The Sermon on the Mount—and almost every teaching in the New Testament—points to a higher existence that only becomes real in God-consciousness, a state of awareness united with the divine.

As a faith, Christianity turned its back on such a radical call to transformation. The Protestant work ethic blatantly contradicts Jesus's teaching not to plan ahead or worry about the future. If Catholicism is tempted to feel pleased because Protestants aren't obeying Christ, how do they live with the most famous lines in the sermon? "You have heard that it was said, 'You shall love your neighbor and hate your enemy.' But I say to you, Love your enemies and pray for those who persecute you, so that you may be children of your Father in heaven" (Matthew 5:43–45). If Catholicism had taken this to heart, there would have been no Inquisition or Crusades in world history.

Loving your enemies reminds me of a story from World War II that always brings tears to my eyes. The Nazis gathered up Jesuit nuns and monks and sent them to the concentration camps, along with Jews, gypsies, and homosexuals. One nun was subjected to the horrifying and perverted medical experiments associated with Dr. Josef Mengele, Auschwitz's dreaded "Angel of Death." The assistant who administered these torments was a woman, one of Mengele's nurses. In extreme suffering, the nun knew she was about to die, and her last act was to take the rosary from her neck. She held it out to the nurse, who recoiled suspiciously and asked what she was doing. The nun replied, "A gift. Take it with my blessing." They were her last words before she died.

Here was a living example of "resist not evil," and in a flash it tells us that Jesus's core teachings depend upon higher consciousness. Few of us could respond to deep, intentional evil with compassion unless, as with this nun, compassion had become part of our nature. In addition, such compassion must replace all that isn't compassionate, those instincts that force us to resist, fight, struggle, and curse evil when it touches our lives.

Jesus was the product of transformation, and he wanted others to be transformed also. Without the process of transformation, Jesus's teachings aren't merely radical. They are impossible to live by (except, of course, in those privileged moments when we find ourselves acting kinder, more loving, and more selfless than usual).

What, then, is the path that Jesus laid out? Parts of it are already familiar. Jesus told his disciples to pray. He asked them to trust in God. They were to rely on faith to accomplish miracles. Their attitude toward the world was to be one of peace and love. Millions of Christians still attempt to live by these precepts, yet something crucial must be missing, because we don't witness a large-scale transformation of human nature among Christians. Like the rest of us, they seem just as tempted to be unloving, violent, selfish, and narrow-minded, the difference being that they are tempted to use their religion to justify their behavior. (In that, they aren't alone—every organized religion creates an ethos that covers over human flaws with self-righteous rhetoric.)

THE MISSING KEY

There's more to the path that Jesus outlined, much of it overlooked because his teaching hasn't been viewed in the light of higher consciousness. Entering the Kingdom of God doesn't mean waiting to die and then joining God. It's an internal event here and now by which human nature turns into something higher. The Sermon on the Mount points to a transformed world that depends upon each individual's following Jesus's guidance. Turning inward seems familiar—every spiritual tradition demands it—but what do we do when we get there? That's the missing key. Speaking in a general way, the process of transformation remains the same today as when Jesus was alive.

Step 1: Shift your perception. The Sermon on the Mount occupies three chapters in the gospel of Matthew and covers many subjects. Yet throughout, Jesus keeps returning to the same general principle: God's reality is the reverse of material reality. That's why the meek shall inherit the earth, why evil shouldn't be resisted, why we should love our enemies. It takes a shift in perception to see this, the same shift that Jesus himself made to arrive at unity with God.

Step 2: God's providence is given to all. When he says that the first shall be last, Jesus isn't referring to the material world, but to the action of grace. Like the rain, mercy falls upon the just and the unjust alike. The birds of the air and the lilies of the field aren't human, but they benefit from Providence, and if we think we must struggle to survive, we don't know God. Being everywhere, God makes himself felt everywhere (it goes without saying that "he" and "she" are interchangeable when speaking of God, and both are inadequate to describe the divine, which has no gender).

Step 3: Go beyond appearances. Your enemy appears to be your enemy, but in God's eyes the two of you are bound by love. To realize this divine equality, you must see beyond gross appearances. The sermon constantly pulls hearers to the soul level, away from the physical.

Step 4: Accept God's love. Jesus constantly seeks to reassure his listeners that they aren't forgotten or alone. They don't have to fight for the necessities of life, and the reason for this is that they are loved. As children of God, they can be denied nothing.

Step 5: See with the eyes of the soul. To live a new way, you have to grasp the opportunities for change. Seeing the world through old expectations and beliefs only reinforces untruth.

In broad sweeps Jesus dismisses all received opinions, even when they have been handed down as the laws of Moses. He wants us to see with a different kind of attention, which comes from the soul.

By using words like "perception" and "attention," I'm emphasizing the way that reality shifts not through actions in the material world, but through actions that occur inside. When Jesus taught that the Kingdom of Heaven is within, he was referring to the mind (or consciousness). When he said that no one can serve two masters, but must chose between God and Mammon, he meant that the claims of the material world—wealth, status, family, power, and possessions—are totally different from the claims of spirit.

The New Testament doesn't lay out a systematic way to enter the Kingdom of Heaven, and so we have to borrow from the great wisdom traditions, Eastern and Western, to fill in the gaps. In almost every tradition, and implicitly in Christianity, reality is divided into three levels: the material, the spiritual, and the divine.

The *material world* is the domain of the body and all physical things. Here we render unto Caesar what is Caesar's; that is, we pay the price, whatever it may be, for daily existence. Because this level of reality is dominated by desire for the good things in life, the pursuit of money, status, power, and possessions puts us in the service of a false god, symbolized by Mammon.

The *Kingdom of God* is the world of spirit, where everything that applies in the material world is turned on its head. Fulfillment isn't a far-off goal, but a given. Events are governed by spiritual laws, and physical limitations no longer exist. Sometimes Jesus calls this level of reality Heaven, and he spends a lot of time enticing people with its rewards. In Heaven everyone will be loved; ceaseless labor will come to an end; a banquet has been prepared for the poor and weak. In Heaven all inequality is banished because no one is a person anymore—everyone is a soul.

God, or *the Absolute,* is the source from which reality is born. It transcends the material world, but being infinite and unbounded, the Absolute goes beyond Heaven also. Christ describes a "peace that passes understanding," meaning that even the mind cannot go here; God's reality is inconceivable.

All three levels penetrate one another. The material world, the Kingdom of God, and God himself are all present at this very moment in you and outside you. To believe that you exist only in the material world is a gross mistake, one that Jesus came to correct. He offered salvation, which opens the door to the two missing dimensions of life, the world of spirit and the source of reality. The reason Jesus makes this seem so effortless ("Knock and the door shall be opened") is that the two lost dimensions have always been here. We just mistakenly perceive that they aren't.

Salvation has a practical benefit. When you realize that the material world is controlled by God, you stop struggling against the obstacles in life. The material world, it turns out, isn't the cause of anything; it's the effect. It receives its signals from the domain of spirit. Each of us receives impulses from the soul, and our thoughts and actions exist to carry them out. Since we do this imperfectly, life turns into a mixture of pleasure and pain. The soul wants only good for us, but that can come about only if the Kingdom of God came to earth, the very thing Jesus aimed for.

Even though the three levels of reality are always present, a person has to rise to higher consciousness to embrace all three worlds. When Jesus said, "I and the Father are one," he indicated that for him it was natural to see everything at once. What did he see? A kind of cascade, beginning with God, flowing downward to the Kingdom of Heaven, and, after filtering through the soul, reaching its final destination in the material world.

Examples will help. Take happiness. Most people believe that external things produce happiness, or at least trigger it. A new car without dents in the fender makes you happier than an old beater with the doors smashed in. More money leads to more happiness through the pleasure it can buy. Constant pleasure, although unattainable, would feel perfect.

But Jesus taught that happiness on earth is a pale reflection of spiritual happiness. The intensity of happiness decreases the further away from God you are. God is pure bliss, a kind of unbounded ecstasy that nothing can diminish or change. This pure bliss cascades down to the Kingdom of Heaven. Here the soul is also ecstatic, but God's bliss must be diminished for human beings to experience it. Therefore, the happiness that pours from the soul becomes conditional. When God's bliss reaches the end of the journey on the material plane, we mistakenly believe that happiness comes and goes. It seems fragile and prone to change. We can be robbed of happiness when things around us go wrong. No longer do we perceive its true source.

THE JOURNEY HOME

Because his eyes were open to the source, Jesus saw reality for what it is: a constant manifestation of God. Why is anything true or beautiful or powerful? Because God contains Truth, Beauty, and Power. It does little good to know this intellectually. Experience is all, and therefore Jesus kept giving such experiences over and over. He performed miracles to show how insubstantial the material world really is. He kept reversing the rules of life to give people a taste of Heaven.

Yet all his teaching was in service of one overarching objective: to find the way back home. To his first Jewish followers, the spiritual history of humans had been one long exile. Adam and Eve were banished from Paradise. The children of Israel were in exile in Egypt and forced into captivity in Babylon. All these disasters were symbolic. They stood for losing sight of the soul and being separated from the Godhead. Speaking simply, Jesus offered Heaven as home and God as the Father who throws a banquet out of joy for the return of all his prodigal sons and daughters.

Jesus knew that God's lost children wouldn't find their way home through a dose of metaphysics. Therefore, he served as an example of someone who was fully physical and spiritual at the same time—God, the soul, and a mortal human being were united. Jesus didn't simply bring the light of God to earth; he was the light. (If it didn't so enrage Christians, I'd call him a guru—the word in Sanskrit means "dispeller of darkness.") When Jesus proclaimed that no one could enter the Kingdom of God except through him, he wasn't referring to an isolated historical person born in Nazareth in the year 1 CE. All uses of "I" by Jesus in the gospels must be taken as God, soul, and human, not because Jesus was unique, but because reality itself fuses all three. (Thus his saying, "Before Abraham was, I am," is Christ's way of pointing to eternity as his ultimate source.)

Now we have a much clearer picture of the path Jesus walked and the one he wants us to walk. Our goal is to shift our allegiance away from the material plane, to be guided by our souls, and ultimately to rejoin our source, which is God. Renunciation of the world, in the sense of giving up on it, has nothing to do with this path, nor does piety and ostentatiously living a religious life in order to seem better than those who don't. Jesus scoffed at all such pretenses and dismissed the professional priestly caste of Pharisees and Sadducees—he called them hypocrites because they knew everything about the letter of God's law, but nothing about its spirit. Not to mention that, like all priests, the Pharisees increased their own status and power by keeping people away from salvation. Protecting their exalted position meant more than showing anyone a path that can be walked individually, without recourse to religious authorities.

I think Jesus's diagnosis, now two thousand years old, is as valid today as ever. Finding a way back home is the core of spiritual existence, indeed of existence itself. How, then, do we heal the separation that makes us feel abandoned by God and isolated from our own souls?

God Is Found Through Transcending

Jesus preached to his disciples that if they found God first, everything else would be added to them. This is our strongest indication that he was pointing not to a father figure sitting on a throne, but to the source of reality. Such a source can't be found through the five senses; it can't be retrieved by thinking about it the way one retrieves a memory. The only path is one of transcendence, or "going beyond."

In Christian tradition there are many forms of going beyond, and believers today continue to practice them. Doing good deeds and giving to charity go beyond selfishness. Praying for the solution to a problem surrenders it to God, going beyond one's own personal efforts. A monk's life sacrifices all material concerns, going beyond any gratification that would satisfy the ego and its unending stream of desires.

Yet I doubt that Jesus had such limited forms of transcendence in mind, because none of them alters reality. God is hidden as if behind a veil. He doesn't speak and is therefore concealed by the thoughts that fill our minds, which never stop speaking. Therefore, transcendence means going beyond the five senses and the mind's constant activity. Here the spiritual world divides, for the West, influenced strongly by Christianity, prefers contemplation of God's divine nature, while the East, influenced by India's ancient spiritual traditions, prefers meditation.

The difference between these two ways of transcending does not have to be so severe, however. In both meditation and contemplation the mind does two things: it quiets down and it expands beyond everyday boundaries. This is accomplished by taking a thought or image and allowing the mind to experience finer and finer states of itself. In mantra meditation, for example, the sound of the mantra gradually grows softer, tapering off into silence. In Christian contemplation of an image, for example, Mary's sacred heart, the image also fades, gaining subtle emotional significance. Meditation tends to be more abstract, since the mantra has no meaning, while contemplation focuses on love, compassion, forgiveness, or some other trait of God.

For many people a less abstract meditation is effective, such as the following meditation on the heart. Sit quietly with your eyes closed. Let your attention go to the center of your chest and without effort keep your mind focused on your heart. Feelings and images are likely to arise, and when they do, softly bring your attention back. Don't force anything; don't resist any emotions or sensations that arise. (Avoid trying to envision the physical heart or detecting your heartbeat—we're speaking of a subtle energy center instead.)

At first this meditation won't yield silence and perhaps not even calm. Everything depends on the state of your heart center, which in most people contains a good deal of conflict. Hidden memories will resurface; repressed emotions will want to flow. Let all of that happen. Soon the experience will shift, as you contact the heart as a center of tenderness and love. Whenever you enter the heart, what you're really seeking is sensitivity. The more sensitive your experience as you meditate, the closer you get to silence. In time, silence will also be transcended, however. It will open the door to an invisible presence. This presence isn't inert. It's very much alive, and the more you sit with it, the more it begins to express attributes of God. Love and tenderness are only two. God is also strong, powerful, all-knowing, boundless, eternal, and uncreated. Your goal is to find the source of all those qualities inside yourself and ultimately to embody them.

The Seeds of Earthly Life Are Planted in Heaven

If you were already in unity with God—the end of the spiritual journey—sitting motionless within your own being would be totally fulfilling. Not because you have escaped this world in a balloon, but because the Absolute, being the source, contains the fulfillment of all desires. When the Lord's Prayer says, "Thine is the kingdom, the power, and the glory," the words indicate the place where all energy, bliss, and creativity come from.

But transcending has many gradations, and it allows you to experience the subtle level of reality, the plane of the soul. At this level of consciousness, unlike the level of the Absolute, or God, there are images, thoughts, and sensations that directly pertain to everyday life. Falling in love at first sight, for example, is like a direct transmission from this subtle realm. So is suddenly knowing the truth about a situation or hitting upon a brilliant solution out of the blue when other ways of solving a problem have failed.

These are only isolated glimpses. The entire subtle realm is within everyone. Here the most desirable things in life—love, creativity, truth, beauty, and power—are planted in seed form, waiting to grow once they enter the physical world. To awaken these seeds, you can practice subtle action, that is, action on the level of the soul. This may sound esoteric, but think about anything you pursue avidly that brings accomplishment and a sense of joy. The following will be present:

Love and enthusiasm

Optimism

Desire to reach a goal

Focused attention

Immunity from distractions

Spontaneous energy

Bursts of fulfillment

Absence of resistance, both inside and out

You can translate these qualities into any object of desire—a lover's pursuit of the beloved, a scientist's cherished research project, a gardener's dream of growing the best roses in the county. None of these activities begins on the physical plane; they begin as seeds in the mind. Activities that we don't pursue, on the other hand, that quickly bore us or simply lack enough momentum to get anywhere, are like stunted seeds. It's not good enough simply to pick up a signal from the soul; you must nourish it and make it part of your life.

What we're talking about here are subtle actions. You can apply them to your spiritual journey with as much ease as you apply them to your beloved, your career, or the Super Bowl, for that matter. The Christian path can be mapped out in terms of subtle actions that are not esoteric; in fact, they are easier to comprehend than traditional religious concepts like grace and faith.

Love and enthusiasm. Find what is lovable in Jesus or, if you are attracted to them, in Mary and the saints. Open yourself to the possibility that God loves you, that you belong in this world in order to have everything a loving father could give. Even if your present reality doesn't permit a wholehearted acceptance of this attitude, open a window. Love is more than a feeling that comes and goes. It's a permanent aspect of your own being, beginning at the source. You are meant to participate in love because you participate in yourself. Keep this vision in mind. Appreciate the most beautiful things in your life, whatever they may be, as expressions of love, gifts that come your way through grace, not by chance or good luck or because you worked hard.

Align yourself with a vision of God as a tree laden with fruit that bows down its branches to bestow some on you. Or think of God as the sun covered by clouds. You don't have to work to find the sun; you only have to wait for the clouds to dissipate. With this vision in mind, it's much easier to be enthusiastic about life, because suddenly the unknown isn't fearful anymore—it's a region from which the next good thing will emerge.

Optimism. Be positive in your expectations. This doesn't have to be merely a mood, and it shouldn't lapse into fantasy. Just be aware that at the soul level the seeds of fruition exist in infinite number. Bad seeds, on the other hand, come from the past, engendered by memory. We remember being hurt and disappointed, and by remaining attached to those bad memories, we keep repeating them. The past plants bad seeds; the mind feeds them with fear and anger.

Optimism focuses on the good seeds. Thus they are given encouragement to sprout. Strictly speaking, I'm not referring to positive thinking. In positive thinking all negative outcomes must be wrenched around until something good comes out of them. In actuality, bad seeds yield bad fruit. But once you face a result that is painful or disappointing, step away from it and focus on the seed of the next situation, which can be a good one. Nobody is perfect at this. We all sprout bad seeds along with the good. However, with an attitude of optimism, you remind yourself to favor the good, and that shift in attention has a powerful influence. (I once knew a mathematical genius and asked him what it was like to think at his level of intelligence. Surprisingly, he said that he hardly thought at all. How, then, I wondered, did he come up with such intricate solutions to math problems? "I ask for the answer, and I expect it to be right," he replied. "When I'm not doing that, my mind is mostly quiet.")

Desire to reach a goal. Many spiritual people are suspicious of desire—if not condemnatory—but desire can work for you on the spiritual path. To do that, it must be focused, and so you need to have a goal in mind. (As a guru once told me, "The wind can't favor your sails until you pick a direction.") Too many people want to be filled with the light (i.e., they want to feel love, delight, fulfillment, and closeness to God) without directing those qualities. God is constantly on the move, because God is just another word for infinite creativity. Genesis occurs at every moment.

If you want to be successful spiritually, prepare to be on the move. The Indian savant J. Krishnamurti expressed this beautifully when he said that true meditation happens twenty-four hours a day. He meant that one should devote one's waking hours to subtle action, finding the most refined way to achieve any goal. Meditation isn't stasis. Silent, unspoken desire has enormous power, especially the power of intention. Direct your mind to a goal and keep focused, asking for reality to unfold in the most fulfilling way. Then let go and watch what happens. Giving over even a tiny desire to God allows you to learn that accomplishment doesn't need to depend on ego-driven struggle. For most of us, it's good to stop at least once a day and consciously resist the urge to interfere. Stand back from the situation—it can be anywhere you are feeling resistance and obstacles—and see if higher consciousness can bring a spontaneous solution. Once you've achieved your first successes, using this same technique becomes effortless and in time a way of life.

Focused attention. In its own right, without any desire in mind, focused attention is one of the mind's most powerful forces. Focused attention is the fertilizer that makes the seeds of the soul come to life. "Seed" is simply a verbal token—what we're really talking about is the potential for a subtle impulse to jump into the physical world and grow Before any piece of matter can emerge—a tree, house, cloud, or mountain range—its atoms exist first as pure potential. This invisible, motionless state then "warms up" into faint vibrations, and those vibrations acquire physicality. (In physics the shift from an invisible, or "virtual," particle into a visible electron is known as the "collapse of the wave function." It's the basic process by which the visible universe becomes manifest, blinking in and out of existence thousands of times a second.)

The same is true of future events in your life. An infinite number of events exist as pure potential. From this unbounded reservoir a select number of possibilities reach the seed stage, which is vibrational. They are waiting in the wings to emerge into physicality. That happens when you turn your mind toward a possibility and say, "Yes, I pick you." Anything that has become important to you in your life followed this transformational route from invisible potential to full-blown event. Therefore, the more focused your attention, the more skilled you can become at activating unseen possibilities (a skill known in the Indian tradition of yoga as "one-pointedness").

Immunity from distractions. A second skill that goes along with focused attention is the ability not to be distracted. You find this ability quite natural when you're in love. Not only do you want to spend every waking thought on your beloved, but outside things also become flat and uninteresting. Avoiding distractions is effortless. In spiritual matters the chief distraction is ego. Being rooted in the physical world, the ego wanders everywhere, consumed by fleeting desires. It is pulled this way and that by fear and expectation. It indulges in fantasies and harbors deep-seated resentments.

The ability of the ego to grab your attention can't be overestimated. After all, the physical world is infinite in its diversity; the five senses never cease to bring new grist for the mill. You can't argue the ego out of its incessant demands for attention, pleasure, self-involvement, success, and winning; therefore, fighting back won't succeed. This is one adversary who must melt away gradually. And what melts it? The higher satisfaction of inner peace, love, calm, and fulfillment, which doesn't need to chase after objects in the physical world. Only transformation quiets the ego and puts it in its place. The best attitude to take while this process unfolds is patience, because gradually, as you experience transformation, the ego will loosen its grip. Keep in mind that "I, me, and mine" aren't the only ways to view life. You can fulfill yourself by living beyond ego, and in time that will happen.

Spontaneous energy. Spirituality isn't about trying. It's about what Buddhists call "nondoing." Jesus expressed the same notion when he taught that life is not something to worry about. The famous passage in the Sermon on the Mount about the birds of the air and the lilies of the field was an illustration of how nature unfolds spontaneously. Life flows; it unfolds without struggle. The energy needed comes without effort.

As a child you dragged your feet going to the dentist and got exhausted if you were saddled with tasks you hated, like mowing the lawn. But when you played, you had unlimited energy. Jesus has the latter state in mind. He wants people not to worry and struggle, because those are the worst ways to be in the world: struggle comes from separation, an inability to let Providence do what it wants to do. Therefore, when you feel spontaneous energy—and not until then—undertake the challenges of life. If, instead, you feel dull, exhausted, depleted, stressed, or simply unenthusiastic, stop and replenish yourself. In this regard the spiritual way of life is also the most practical, because it taps into the source of spontaneous energy. If you have the courage to live the life you love, all the better.

Bursts of fulfillment. It may be part of the Protestant work ethic to postpone gratification, and Aesop's fable predicts woe for the grasshopper and wealth for the ant. Even so, Jesus held exactly the opposite view. Life doesn't wait for fulfillment tomorrow. It expresses fulfillment today. In the state of separation this sounds delusional. Therefore, as a reminder that the world's way isn't God's way, resist the urge to control, plan, postpone, and hoard.

All of these activities make time your enemy. God is timeless, and so are you. The timeless waits for nothing. It doesn't resign itself to dullness today in hopes of brightness tomorrow. Every occasion for a burst of satisfaction should be seized. When you see something beautiful, appreciate it.

When you feel a loving impulse, say something to the one you love. Be generous each and every time you can. Withhold no good impulse. You may fear that you will run to excess and squander too much, but those feelings are born of fear. In God's reality, the more you give of yourself—in feeling, generosity, self-expression, goodness, creativity, and love—the more you will be given.

Absence of resistance, both inside and out. And then there's the Adversary. You must take into account those invisible forces that resist God, that deny fulfillment and extinguish love. There's no need to attribute such obstacles to the Devil or malignant fate. The truth is that human beings are entangled in the drama of good and bad, light and dark. Opposition fuels creation; there's no getting around it. But this recognition is very different from feeling obliged to fight the darkness, either within or without. We are so addicted to struggle, not to mention war and violence, that we scarcely register Jesus's dictum, "Resist not evil." Yet evil itself puts up massive resistance; it is futile to adopt the same tactic.

The spiritual attitude in all things is to accept and say yes. The seeds of the soul grow in mysterious directions. You can never foretell when a temporary obstacle will lead to future good. "Everything happens for a reason" is a useful reminder of this. And yet pain and distress are not acceptable; being denied what you deeply desire is not an occurrence you should resign yourself to. Therefore, saying yes and offering no resistance cannot be taken as an iron rule. It goes without saying that push does in fact come to shove, and in those situations people fight, struggle, and practice violence. And when evil is conquered, however temporary the victory, something good has prevailed, perhaps God.

Even so, the higher way is not to offer resistance, to see if a peaceful way can be found. This leads to a general guide that sums up much of what has gone before. In any situation, when you find yourself acting in a certain way, observe what's happening and apply three questions:

Do I feel fulfilled and happy acting this way?

Is it easy for me?

Has it brought the right results?

Simple as they sound, these questions encapsulate much of Jesus's teaching. God intends for life to proceed easily; he wants us to experience fulfillment; he intends for the seeds of the soul to flourish as naturally as the grasses of the field.

At any given moment, measure your existence by the same standard. Life is too complex to master one situation at a time. The future unfolds too unexpectedly to allow for dress rehearsals. So you must acquire the skill of living here and now, and the greatest skill comes from the level of the soul. Reality cascades from the divine to the mundane, and yet by some miracle even the mundane is divine. The same miracle brings joy in the vale of tears and immortality in the shadow of death. It's not easy to extract one from the other. Therefore, we constantly need inspired teachers like Jesus. It would be a shame to be shown such sublime truth and not take advantage of it every waking moment.

PHOTO BY JEREMIAH SULLIVAN

DEEPAK CHOPRA is the author of more than fifty books translated into over thirty-five languages, including numerous *New York Times* bestsellers in both the fiction and nonfiction categories. Chopra's Wellness Radio airs weekly on Sirius Stars, Channel 102, which focuses on the areas of success, love, sexuality and relationships, well-being, and spirituality. He is founder and president of the Alliance for a New Humanity. *Time* magazine heralds Deepak Chopra as one of the top 100 heroes and icons of the century and credits him as "the poet-prophet of alternative medicine."

www.deepakchopra.com